Catholic Christianity
in Evolution

T0373365

Catholic Christianity in Evolution

The Spiritual Prophecy of Teilhard de Chardin

ALAN B. SAGE

sussex
ACADEMIC
PRESS
Brighton • Chicago • Toronto

2 4 6 8 10 9 7 5 3 1

First published in 2021 in Great Britain by
SUSSEX ACADEMIC PRESS
PO Box 139
Eastbourne BN24 9BP

Distributed in North America by
SUSSEX ACADEMIC PRESS
Independent Publishers Group
814 N. Franklin Street
Chicago, IL 60610

British Library Cataloguing in Publication Data
A CIP catalogue record for this book is available from the British Library.

Library of Congress Cataloging-in-Publication Data
To be applied for.

Paperback ISBN 978-1-78976-131-3

Typeset & designed by Sussex Academic Press, Brighton & Eastbourne.
Printed by TJ Books Ltd, Padstow, Cornwall.

Contents

Acknowledgements

I would like to thank my family and all those who have encouraged me in writing this book, most especially my wife Mary and my sister Celia for their continued love and support and Dr. John Kusel for his friendship and intellectual stimulus.

Catholic Christianity in Evolution

Introduction

This small book has been gradually forming in my mind for some years and has now reached a stage of readiness for publication. It represents the conclusions of reflections over the past 50 years or so on theology and spirituality in the Church and I hope that it will find an echo in your own experience and aspirations, providing a basis for further development of your own thinking and practice.

Although written from a Roman Catholic perspective I hope it will be of use and interest to Christians in other traditions. It is written for the many people in the Church who want to enrich their understanding of faith and spirituality; it is not an academic work, although it includes discussion of theological and scientific themes, so references and academic discussion have been kept to a minimum in the hope that it will reach as many as possible. As will become evident in the pages that follow, my thinking has been greatly influenced by the French Jesuit Pierre Teilhard de Chardin, a constant companion in my theological and spiritual journey. His significance will become clear in the pages that follow.

In recent years we have seen church congregations diminishing and the church's message becoming less effective for many in today's world. In order to try and make the message more relevant Pope Benedict initiated a new evangelism programme which had some effect within the church but did little to attract those outside the church, those who were the main audience to be reached; Pope Francis has taken up this task with a much more attractive message which has clearly outlined a vision of Catholic Christianity which fully embraces the world and its needs and aspirations and emphasises the importance of concern for the poor, disadvantaged and disenfranchised people in a world often dominated by purely economic considerations. Allied to this is an awareness of creation as the primary gift of God and the responsibility of all to care for this gift and ensure that it is used for the benefit of the whole of humanity. Finally, Pope Francis has also highlighted the notion of church as the servant of humanity and its need to be concerned not so much for itself and its own dignity but for its humble service to others. He speaks of the church as primarily a missionary church, taking the joy of the Gospel to the world at large and he points out that every Christian is challenged, here and now, to be actively engaged in evangelization – every Christian is a missionary. The Pope is clearly indicating that the aspiration to personal holiness can only be fulfilled within the context of our missionary calling and reaching out to others in need whoever and wherever they may be.

Our spiritual life starts with the initiative of God's love in our hearts and grows and develops as we share this love with others. What is clear is that Christian life is not a kind of sheltered enclosure where we commune with God as it were separate from the world. Pope Francis speaks of Christians getting their hands dirty, being involved in the daily lives of others, especially those at the fringes of human society, the poor, the suffering, the aged and the outcasts of society such as addicts, prisoners and migrants. In prayer and worship we sanctify and offer to God all our efforts for others. This is the 'sacrament of the brother', so dear to the heart and message of Pope Francis.

However, despite this new approach taken by the Pope, and his stress on the importance of creation in God's design, the realm of spirituality is still formed within a predominantly redemptive theology rather than a fully creation-centred context and also within a static view of the world rather than in a dynamic and evolutionary setting. What is needed, therefore, is a broader Christian vision, seen within an evolutionary, dynamic world-view context which is the way in which science and much of today's thinking understands our world.

In this book I will try to outline what Christian life within an evolutionary, changing world looks like and thus amplify and enrich the vision given us by Pope Francis. In this task I will be led by the thinking of a man who has been a large influence on Pope Francis, his Jesuit confrere Pierre Teilhard de Chardin, whose vision of Christian living takes some of the themes of the Pope and puts them into a wider and more conducive context, making Christian life and faith much more amenable to contemporary modes of thinking. Although from a different time and with a very different background to Pope Francis, he shares with him the Ignatian theme of 'finding God in all things' and a concern to make Christian faith and life of contemporary relevance. Where he adds a new dimension to the

Pope's teaching is in his cosmic approach to redemption and the notion of ongoing divine creativity; Pope Francis does, in fact, make a positive reference to this aspect of Teilhard's thinking in his encyclical *Laudato Si'*, but does not develop it in any extensive fashion.

Although this is not a book of history, I do refer to the history of theology in the Church in order to highlight some of the important themes that form part of our understanding of the Gospel message. Down the centuries there have always been different ideas and emphases in the Church's thinking which enriches the appreciation of the mystery of Christ. I have paid some attention to thinking in the 20th century in Chapter 3 because it was a time of rich development which came to a head in the documents of the Second Vatican Council. The dates and details of the theologians encountered are not of importance as such and it is rather the ideas and insights that they offer which are my main focus. What they do is to remind us of various aspects of our faith which form the rich and multi-layered insights into our faith in God, Christ and our life as Christians today. Hopefully, this brief survey will give you some topics for reflection as you reflect on your own experience of faith.

I will begin, in Chapter One, with some general, introductory thoughts on what it means for us as Christians and the kind of world we are living in and the new challenges evolution presents. This will be followed by a brief introduction to Teilhard de Chardin, outlining his main concerns which he first presented in an essay written in 1919 entitled: Note on the Presentation of the Gospel in a New Age, a truly prophetic writing which grasped fully the needs of evangelisation in the modern world (Chapter Two). This will frame our discussion of the needs for a modern, relevant vision for evangelisation and Christian living today.

In Chapters Three to Five I will consider the way in which our thinking and theology have changed in the past 50 years or so (Chapter 3), the question of God's creativity and the way we look at the world in an evolutionary context (Chapter Four) and the implications of these changes for church organisation, worship and practice (Chapter Five)

In Chapter Six, I introduce Teilhard the man and how he saw his life and mission. Chapter Seven will provide a more extended explanation of Teilhard's vision, in particular his approach to

Christian living, which he dealt with in his book *The Divine Milieu* in 1927. Here he provides a practical guide to being a Christian in the world, with his emphasis on 'living in the divine milieu' and 'building God's world', which bring alive our relationship to God and our active part in making God's gift of creation a continuing reality.

Finally, in Chapter Eight I will bring together some of the many strands covered in the chapters to provide a brief overview of a spirituality for today, incorporating the insights of the theologians of the last century, including Teilhard, and the documents of Vatican II.

In the Appendix: Reading Teilhard, I offer an opportunity for those who wish to further or deepen their understanding of Teilhard with a guided approach to his view of The Christian in the World. Originally, I intended to include the relevant texts from Teilhard's writings; however, due to issues of copyright I have been unable to do this. Instead, I have given references for these texts so that you can follow them up. I appreciate that some of the volumes of his writings may not be easily available in libraries or bookshops, though many used copies are available on Amazon; however, *The Divine Milieu* and *The Human Phenomenon* are available in the original editions and in new translations (published by Sussex Academic Press). In the References at the end of the book I have given a list of all his published volumes along with abbreviations for the volumes and the individual essays.

In order to add to an understanding of some of the ideas discussed, I have included a Glossary of selected words which will, hopefully, broaden your awareness and appreciation of Teilhard's theological and spiritual vision. You will notice that Teilhard often uses Latin phrases to emphasise certain terms or ideas; I have given a translation of these where required.

CHAPTER ONE

Living in a Changing World
Challenges and Rewards

If we are to be a successful missionary Church we have to show the significance of Christian human endeavour to the future of the universe and the whole human community and to point up the role of the Church and the Christian community in this God-given task. This entails an understanding of the world we live in and how this has changed from a static to an evolutionary viewpoint.

When Christianity developed in the early centuries, the idea of an evolving universe was unthinkable; the world was seen as a static reality, unchanging, like God its creator. Nothing changed because God was unchangeable, forever the same. In this respect, God was totally other or transcendent. In this picture the earth tended to be seen as just the backdrop to the drama of human salvation and didn't have meaning in itself but was put there merely for us humans to work out our way to heaven, despite talk of the beauty of God's world. Along with this view, there was the notion of the Great Chain of being in which there is an ascending movement up from the lower regions of the earth, up through humanity and on into the spheres of the angelic and heavenly world up to the realm of the divine. This was seen as a movement from the material up through the spiritual to God.

The concept of God was the result of reflection on the scriptural revelation, both in the Old and New Testaments, and input from the Platonic philosophical world view which was the background within which the early Christian thinkers developed their ideas and tried to communicate their faith vision to the world around them. In some ways, this philosophy emphasised the spiritual notion of God and made God much more remote than the scriptures might suggest. For Plato and his followers, this world we live in is not the ultimately real world but an image or reflection of the real world in the mind of God.

The implications of this world view was to emphasise the priority of the spiritual over the material spheres of our experience and separate our spiritual life from our everyday life. This became the basic Christian attitude for future Christian history and inevitably included an element of anti-material attitudes which became clear in the predominance of monastic forms of spirituality and a neglect of the spiritual needs of ordinary Christians. These attitudes were further developed by St Augustine and his influence on the future was highly significant; his views on sexuality further substantiated an anti-material bias in Christian life which has continued up to the present day. Thus, we have been left with a heritage of Christian spirituality which struggles, with a form of split personality in which there is a tension between our everyday concerns and responsibilities and our spiritual or prayer life which for many is viewed as the more important of the two – God is more important than the world. This tension is too distracting for many and becomes the reason for abandoning the spiritual quest in a church context and looking for alternatives which may offer a more unitive approach to faith life or completely opting out of faith in God. What is needed is a form of Christian humanism, which affirms creation and the world as the gift of God and the consequent responsibility of Christians to fully engage with the world and work for its redemption rather than observe it, as it were, from the outside in a detached fashion. There were, however, efforts to counter the monastically based forms of spirituality and provide support for lay people living in the world. During the 15th century the Brothers of the Common Life, a lay community, set out to make spirituality a central element of people's lives and were instrumental in the writing of The Imitation of Christ by Thomas a Kempis, a spiritual classic that has been a vade mecum for lay people right up into the present day. It is a book for everyday Christian living and not for the spiritual elite or monks and religious; however, it still shows a certain fear of 'the world' and its distractions. The notion of the world, of course, has its origin in the scriptures, where it presents as a largely distractive force against faith and spirituality. St John's epistles speak about the world and appear to counsel wariness about succumbing to its wiles, though for John the world may represent all those gentiles who, like the Jews, failed to accept Jesus; we also need to understand that the world is spoken of both in its redeemed and unredeemed state and so should not be automatically steered clear of it as though it is always a bad influence. Jesus speaks a lot about interior attitude in our life but also speaks about contact with the world; he speaks about the beauty of nature and God's care for it and also turns our intention to everyday living and the lives of others as where we need to recognise God. For Jesus the world is where we meet God and others; we cannot turn our back on the world but must embrace it as the place where God speaks to us and God's values must become incarnated.

At the time of the Reformation, there was a great impulse to make faith a living reality for everyone and to break down barriers between priests/monks and ordinary people and allow access to the scriptures to everyone. This was embraced within the various Protestant communities but less so within the Roman Church; however, there were some in this church who took a similar approach. Desiderius Erasmus, at one time an Augustinian monk like Martin Luther, was a biblical scholar, made a new translation of the Greek New Testament and was an advocate of a form of Christian humanism and wrote a small book of spiritual advice for lay people, *The Handbook for the Christian Soldier*, at the request of the wife of a soldier. In this book he encouraged involvement in worldly affairs and offered words of advice, including scriptural reading. While this book would still not be fully appropriate to us today, it was a step in the right direction and took lay spirituality seriously. In subsequent centuries, Catholic spirituality made little progress, apart from some efforts from people such as St Francis de Sales and St Alphonsus Liguori who both recognised the need for a spirituality which was appropriate to the lay state. However, it was not until the 20th century that a true lay spirituality began to be developed and, perhaps not unsurprisingly, this was started in monastic communities especially in Belgium and France. We shall return to this movement later when we survey the changes in liturgical and theological thinking during that century, and I will start with one of the most important but largely unnoticed initiatives made at the very beginning of the 1900s. This is where I introduce Pierre Teilhard de Chardin, who is very much my inspiration in writing this book and who has influenced most of my thinking over the past 50 years. In the next chapter I will very briefly outline Teilhard's contribution to the issue.

CHAPTER TWO

A Prophetic Voice
Teilhard and Evangelism

Pierre Teilhard de Chardin (usually called Teilhard and pronounced Teyar) was a Jesuit priest and a scientist (palaeontology) who, shortly after entering academic life was called up to service in the First World War and became a stretcher bearer at the front for which he was later awarded a bravery medal. During the war Teilhard was close to his soldier colleagues, worked, suffered and prayed with them; his war service had a tremendous effect on his life and writing. Rather surprisingly, during periods of rest between times of battle he wrote his first essays and these reflected both his prayer life and his human and Christian experience. He was of a mystical disposition and his writing in his earlier essays is suffused with a lyrical, poetic form of expression which is not found to the same extent in his later writings, where his scientific mind is much more apparent. His first essay, "Cosmic Life" (1916), is an instant reminder of his form of spirituality and his theological approach – rooted in the world and not remote from everyday concerns. We will look more at his writing and thinking later but here look at an early essay in which he sets out the basic elements of his vision which he would develop in detail throughout the rest of his life.

When he wrote his essay (Note on the Presentation of the Gospel in a New Age) in 1919 he was acutely aware of the sterility of the current Roman Catholic theology of God and creation. As a scientist and working with many who were closed to religious belief, he was conscious of the need for the Church to engage with the world and to present a message which would find an echo in people's everyday experience. For Teilhard, if the church were to present a credible message to the world of his day it needed to offer a more attractive and inspiring Gospel vision. He laid down three areas where change was required – theology, morality and spirituality – and summed up the vision which he was later to expand in greater detail in the many volumes of his writings. As we shall have to note later, he was not allowed to openly publish his writings during his life due to prohibition by church authorities and it was only after his death in 1955 that they would see the full light of day in openly published form. But more about that later. What was his prescription for a renewed Gospel message? He began with the following words:

> "So long as we appear to wish to impose on the men of today a ready-made Divinity from outside . . . we shall inevitably be preaching in the desert. There is only one way of enthroning God as sovereign over the men of our time: and that is to embrace the ideal they reach out to; it is to seek, with them, the God whom we already possess but who is as yet amongst us as though he were a stranger to us." (HM/NPG 210–11)

His main point here is that our concept of God is too remote from our experience and therefore has little meaning for us. What he suggests, therefore, is a new concept or understanding of God.

> "The God for whom our century is waiting must be:
> 1. As vast and mysterious as the Cosmos.
> 2. As immediate and all-embracing as Life.
> 3. As linked (in some way) to our effort as Mankind."
> (HM/NPG 212)

What he is saying here is that we need to bring God closer to creation and humanity and not envisage God as a remote, ethereal being who is totally other but rather as at the very heart of the creative process. This requires us to re-think creation, not as a once and for all event in the past but as a continuing process in which God is still creating and is the energy or force which underpins everything that happens. In this way God comes nearer to us and takes on a fuller meaning in our everyday life.

In addition to this re-imagining of God, Teilhard goes on in the essay to draw out some of the implications of this new concept of God in our attitude to Christian faith and living. If God is still active in creation we need to cooperate in this ongoing work as co-creators with God. In this way we help God to bring the divine work to fulfilment. This is both an awesome privilege but also a tremendous responsibility; this makes literally everything we do as of saving significance and thus fulfilling as a human being. Teilhard speaks of this as the Gospel of human effort, which became the core of his later work The Divine Milieu. He was convinced that unless we are able to give full meaning to our human work as Christians then we would continue to experience dissatisfaction as both humans and as Christians; there needs to be an integration of all our activity into the sphere of God. He speaks about living in the divine milieu where everything finds its meaning and significance in God. Thus, spirituality is not a separate compartment in our life, divorced from our everyday concerns, but about meeting God in all that we do. Similarly, Christian morality should be concerned not just with individual responsibilities but also about social and communal, even global issues. We will revisit many of these topics later, but this early essay clearly provides a template for a new Christian vision. What is amazing is that this was written in 1919, how prophetic it was; what is disappointing is that his message was dismissed as being not in accord with Catholic teaching and not of benefit to the many people who were looking for meaning in their lives at a time of great suffering. Perhaps this is not surprising and that as often happens people of vision are viewed as misguided and a danger to society. At that time, Roman Catholicism was emerging from the Modernist era and any deviation from what was viewed as the norm was considered dangerous. Unfortunately, this attitude continued up into the latter part of the twentieth century and as a result Teilhard was under censure right up until his death. Despite these obstructions Teilhard's insights fortunately found many willing listeners and his influence grew and provided an impetus for others to develop his ideas. We will return to his ideas later.

CHAPTER THREE

A Century of Change in Church and World

This is not meant to be a history lesson but it is important to understand the new attitudes to the world and to spirituality which developed during the 20th century and which were glimpsed in Teilhard's writings and gradually became part of the thinking and practice of the Church.

What we find during the 20th century is the gradual transformation of Catholic theology and thinking towards a more inclusive vision and the framing of the faith within the context of a changing world, a world that had experienced two World Wars which had devastating effects on people's lives but also led to new and more hopeful aspirations.

Here we can merely provide a brief overview of the movements and individuals responsible for the changes that were to take place but it is important to see them as a gradual effort to reformulate Catholic thinking and practice in response to a changing world which needed a new spiritual and moral underpinning in its efforts to meet the challenges of a new era.

Reform Movements

There were a number of movements which emerged within Church circles, often as a result of challenges from outside the Catholic community and which acted as spurs to action and change. Perhaps one of the most significant was the Biblical Movement, which was precipitated by developments within biblical scholarship in the Protestant communities, namely the rise of biblical criticism which aimed to use the tools of literary and historical studies to understand the scriptures more fully and effectively. There was an initial rejection of much of this work from Catholic thinkers but scholars such as the French Dominican Père Lagrange gradually began to frame a Catholic response which led to the development of a more positive approach to Catholic scriptural studies, underlined by the encyclical Providentissimus Deus of Pope Leo XIII (1893) which laid down principles for scriptural interpretation within a Catholic framework. A Pontifical Biblical Commission was formed in 1902 whose aim was to encourage and support catholic scholars in their task. Further papal guidance was forthcoming in later encyclicals such as Pope Pius XII's *Divino Afflante Spiritu* in 1943. At the same time, there was a growing awareness within the church that the biblical text was not openly available to the Catholic faithful other than through official liturgical texts. In order to make the Bible more easily available, new translations were produced such as *La Sainte Bible* emanating from the Dominican Biblical School in Jerusalem, which would be the basis for the new English translation, the Jerusalem Bible, in the early 1960s.

At the same time, there was a growing awareness of the need for more active participation by lay people in the church's liturgy, particularly the eucharist; not only the Bible but the prayers and texts of the mass began to appear in vernacular languages. Dom Gaspar Lefebvre, a Benedictine monk in the Abbey of St André in Bruges, Belgium produced the first Daily Missal between 1920 and 1951, which became The St Andrews Missal in English; other writers engaged in offering texts and commentaries on the mass and other liturgical ceremonies, including Fr Pius Parsch, the Czech liturgist who provided reflection on biblical themes and readings from the Sunday masses. Through these and other publications lay people were supported and encouraged to take a more active part in the church's liturgy and enrich their spiritual lives.

Pope Pius XII gave an important impetus to studies and practice of the liturgy with his encyclical Mediator Dei in 1947 and later in the 1950s he introduced some simplifications in the Easter ceremonies, and this process was continued and brought to greater fruition with the publication of the Document on the Liturgy at Vatican II which led to a more participative form of liturgical celebration and the extensive use of vernacular languages.

While much was taking place within the practice of faith in the Church, relationships with others outside the Church were also developing. From an era during which Christians from other churches and people of non-Christian faiths were regarded with at least suspicion if not fear, there was a gradual awareness of the similarities as well as the differences that existed between people of different faith traditions, especially non-catholic Christians. Two World Wars had had significant influences on the way in which people viewed others from different nations and parts of the world. War inevitably forges close relationships with one's neighbours, a shared experience of fear and civic restrictions. Not surprisingly, these experiences had repercussions for inter church relationships and over time there was a gradual weakening of traditional hostility and suspicion. Theologians such as Yves Congar, who wrote the first book on ecumenism by a Roman Catholic theologian in 1939 (*Divided Christendom*), were instrumental in changing attitudes towards those of other faiths. These initial efforts would bear fruit in warming approaches within Vatican circles to those outside the Church, particularly under the leadership of the great Jesuit Cardinal Bea who was also an important biblical scholar in his own right.

Shared biblical scholarship, of course, had led to much greater understanding among theologians and biblical scholars, and together with a more united world began to change attitudes of Catholics to other Christians and later to non-Christians. This process culminated in Vatican II's Decree on Ecumenism and Declaration on Non-Christian Religions.

So, we see during the course of the early 20th century the emergence of several movements within the church which aimed to meet the challenges of a changing world. Biblical studies were at first something of a battleground between Catholic and Protestant scholars but gradually became a ferment of renewal and cooperation, leading to greater appreciation of the place of the scriptures in Christian life and, in turn, leading to a richer and more inclusive theology. At the same time, access to the scriptures led to closer collaboration among Christians and a greater appreciation of the similarities in faith as opposed to an emphasis on differences. Liturgical renewal, of course, went hand in hand with an emphasis on the centrality of the scriptures in worship and Christian living and in this way a new form of Christian spirituality began to emerge which was both biblically rooted but also firmly wedded to a positive attitude to the needs and challenges of the modern world.

Theological Renewal

At the same time as the biblical, liturgical and ecumenical movements were gaining ground and influencing attitudes and practice among clergy and laity, the fabric of the faith was being reappraised and reshaped by the theologians and thinkers in the Church, providing a new vision for Christianity in the new, quickly changing world. Although not a professional theologian Teilhard de Chardin wrote on many theological topics and in his many essays was to raise issues and present a new context for theological thinking which others were able to develop and extend. In this respect Teilhard had an indirect but very important influence on the framing of a new theology.

As mentioned earlier, one of the first directly theological essays Teilhard wrote was "Note on the Presentation of the Gospel in a New Age". Basically, Teilhard advocates a new concept of God which emphasises the immanence of God, the fact that God is at the very centre of the evolutionary movement in the cosmos and within the world process rather than outside as an almost disinterested onlooker. Secondly Teilhard proposes a spirituality which embraces the world and its concerns rather than advocating withdrawal from the world, in other words a form of Christian humanism.

What becomes clear is that the world is not just a place of trial or a backdrop to our salvation and redemption. If we consider God as creator of all things then literally everything has an innate meaning and value. This is the very essence of Teilhard's vision.

Looking at the broader developments within theology, along with the insights of Teilhard, we see the gradual emergence of a richer Christian vision which would give the impetus for Pope John XXIII to embark on his calling of a Council to provide a new Catholic vision for the modern world.

Here I would like to very briefly introduce some of the thinkers and ideas which were part of this preparation for Vatican II, which will help to provide a wider picture for our consideration of spirituality and Christian living.

Just prior to World War Two, the Jesuit Émile Mersch wrote extensively on the theme of the Mystical Body and in doing so sowed the seeds of a new way of understanding the nature of the church as a community of people rather than as a hierarchical institution. The Italian born but German speaking Romano Guardini made a huge contribution to our understanding of the person of Jesus Christ in his two major works *The Lord* and *The Humanity of Christ*, both of which were hugely influential in thinking about Jesus as a human, as the model for humanity. Previously Jesus was largely seen as the Christ-God and the role of his humanity was rarely emphasised. What Guardini did was to turn our attention to the importance of the humanity of Christ in his redemptive role. It is precisely in his humanity that Jesus incarnates the divine, that God truly entered the historical course of creation. Guardini was also an advocate for a more participative liturgy and in many ways a trail blazer of the liturgical movement.

One other theologian of note during the early years was the liturgical scholar Josef Jungmann who provided the basis for a historical appreciation of the development of the mass in the Roman Rite. But he was also deeply involved in Christian education or catechesis and wanted to present the Good News as a positive and joyful message rather than a set of dry theoretical statements and he developed what came to be known as kerygmatic theology, harking back to the gospel kerugma or preaching which emphasised both the newness and positive character of Jesus' message. His work in this area was the forerunner of what we know today as catechetics.

The French Dominican Yves Congar was a historian of theology and thus had a handle on the course of theological thinking down the ages and the different ways in which Catholic faith was understood and presented in response to the various challenges that history threw up, including the Reformation and the rise of science and rationalism. He is best known, however, for his contribution to ecclesiology, the theology of the church, and relationships of the church to other Christians and religious traditions or ecumenism. Congar had been a prisoner at Colditz and was very deeply influenced by his war time experience, leading to a more eirenic approach to inter church relationships and a strong emphasis on personal and communal experience within Christian living. He also penned one of the first books on the place of the laity in the church, *Lay People in the Church*, and informed much of the thinking about the nature of the church at Vatican II, where the concepts of the People of God and the Mystical Body were emphasised as prior to the notion of a hierarchical community. What is impressive about Congar's work and writing is its incarnational emphasis; his writing comes from his experience of living within the church community in different times and places and is about this lived experience. He was an advocate for an inclusive and open church, far from the triumphalism of the past. He also called for a renewal of power structures in the church and for a church of and for the poor. As a historian he made a distinction between tradition as the essence of the church's life and traditions as particular, historical expressions of this essence which could and should change in response to new situations of being in the world. Finally, Congar speaks about the importance of a listening church, the importance of prayer and listening to the Spirit; this entails a church of dialogue, a church in which all are recipients of God's Spirit and in which 'the world' is not an enemy but a reality to be embraced and open to the workings of the Spirit. One could sum up Congar's Christian vision as one of openness, hope, personal commitment and mutual trust.

Developments in biblical theology were brought to fruition in a very tangible fashion by the French Redemptorist Francis Xavier Durrwell in his truly ground-breaking book *The Resurrection*. Prior to this time the resurrection was, in most theological manuals, presented as a scriptural proof for the divinity of Jesus rather than as the pinnacle of the saving activity of Jesus and in this respect they presented a truncated form of the Christian message. In Durrwell's writings the resurrection is seen as the culmination of the redemptive work of Christ and thus central to Christian faith; it pointed to the importance of the eucharist as a celebration of the risen Christ as we are reminded by the early church communities meeting weekly on "the eighth day" to celebrate the Risen Lord. In terms of the eucharist, of course, it is a reminder that in communion we receive the Risen Lord and not the Christ of Calvary; in turn, this has implications for the concept of the real presence and the notion of sacrifice. In relation to Christian spirituality, this new emphasis on the resurrection leads to a more joyful celebration of the eucharist and a more forward-looking spiritual attitude, anticipating the Parousia and the fulfilment of creation in Christ as emphasised by St Paul in his cosmic texts and clearly enunciated in Teilhard's development of Pauline Christology.

Other theologians expanded this vision to embrace the whole sacramental order, the presence of Christ in the sacraments of the church and the importance of the sacraments as signs and symbols of the divine presence not only in the church and sacraments but in the whole created order. The Flemish Dominican Eduard Schillebeeckx shows how God's presence in the world is expressed at different levels of clarity and expression, from vague sentiments of the divine in the human psychological make-up, through the sense of God in nature to the sacramental presence in the sacraments and especially the eucharist. It is in the person of Jesus Christ that God's presence finds its most perfect expression and in sending his Spirit Christ inaugurates the church as the continuation of the presence of Christ. So, we live in a sacramental universe, which is accentuated in the sacramental life of the liturgy. An important element of the sacraments, of course, is their use of symbolism, and the combination of word and action. Thus, in the eucharist the Word of God is equally as important as the Eucharistic action, a point made very forcefully in the Decree on Divine Revelation and also in the Constitution on the Liturgy of Vatican II, an important message in regard to the celebration of the eucharist as a complete action in which word and action complement each other.

Schillebeecx also wrote two important books, on Jesus the Christ and Mary, Mother of the Redeemer. What he presents is a very real Jesus who became the Christ and the importance of the humanity of Christ as revealed in the Gospel message. In his work on Mary he provides a very balanced view of her place in the church and in the life of the individual Christian. He shows how Mary was one of the redeemed and in this sense on our side rather than on the side of Christ in terms of her relationship to God. While she has a very important role in the work of redemption as mother of Jesus, she herself is one of the redeemed and it is to Christ that we must first turn as our redeemer and not to Mary. This counterbalanced some of the previous inclinations in Catholic theology to speak of Mary as Mediatrix of all graces as though she was responsible for our salvation rather than Christ the sole redeemer.

The German Jesuit Karl Rahner, hailed by many as the greatest theologian since Thomas Aquinas, set the tone for the latter part of the 20th century, with his breadth and innovative insights. One of the things that Rahner emphasised was the need for an inclusivity in Catholic thinking and an awareness that the Catholic Church did not have all the answers and had to be open to insights from outside its fold, even in the secular sphere. He also speaks of the sacramental universe, the fact that creation displays traces of its divine origin in different ways and at different levels; Christ is THE sacrament of God and his presence in the church and sacraments is the highest manifestation of this presence we can experience and the eucharistic presence is the fullest expression of this.

One of the most significant elements of Rahner's thinking is the insight he offers on the place of Christ in our understanding of humanity. For the most part we look at humanity, make some assumptions about its nature and then, as it were, 'tag on' what we know of Jesus in his humanity as additional information and make Jesus a super-human. Rahner turns this process on its head and suggests that we start with Jesus as THE human person, the exemplar of humanity, and then work down to a notion of what humanity is or might be. Jesus thus becomes the basis of what it means to be human and provides the blueprint for human personality and its development in each individual. This approach makes Christ and the Christian message central to the whole human enterprise rather than something at the periphery, or worse, immaterial to human life. Furthermore, it also makes it evident that Christianity has something to offer the world and its message can provide insight and direction for the human task and is central to what we are trying to achieve in the human community. Rahner then takes this a stage further and suggests that the core of Christian belief is already present in some way in the contours of human nature, if only in a nascent or indeterminate fashion. He speaks of the 'anonymous Christian' to designate this feature, the fact that expressions of basic Christian values and an acknowledgement of the divine presence are to be found in many ways of living and belief. There is, then, a basis for dialogue between Christianity and those of different or no faith. The presence of God is to be found in many forms and at different levels of intensity and realism. Christians believe that the fullest form of expression is to be found in the person and message of Christ and, by extension, his church.

Henri De Lubac, the French Jesuit who was at the heart of theological renewal and was made a Cardinal shortly before he died as a recognition of his contribution to theology, was also a friend and advocate of Teilhard de Chardin and wrote several books explaining Teilhard's thinking, supporting him in his difficulties with Church authorities. One of his most important contributions to the theological debate was that of ' the supernatural existential', which in some ways complemented Rahner's anonymous Christianity. De Lubac suggests that the whole of creation and humanity exist within a supernatural order. Whereas it was traditionally held that there are two orders, one natural and another supernatural, as it were superimposed on it, De Lubac says that there was never a time when there was a purely natural state but that the whole creative venture is subject to a supernatural purpose from the very beginning. In this respect the notion of a natural state is a purely theoretical notion used to emphasize the importance of the supernatural. Contrary to those who accused De Lubac of denying the concept of the supernatural and the grace and influence of God, he sees it as enhancing creation and humanity as part of God's plan right from the start and also points out that this plan can only finally brought to fulfilment through the action of God. In this particular issue we find clear evidence of Teilhard's possible influence on De Lubac. Teilhard was thinking along these lines as early as 1920 when he began to discuss the impact of evolution on the concept of original sin and the Fall of humanity, where he clearly finds difficulty in accepting the notion of a natural, pre-Fall state of humanity in an evolutionary world.

On the question of grace and sin which was another area in need of re-definition, two Dutch theologians, Piet Fransen and Piet Schoonenberg, both highly influenced by Teilhard, wrote particularly on this topic and on the place of Christ in the history of salvation and Christian spirituality. Their focus on Christ was very much concerned with seeing him within the context of evolution and reconciling biblical perspectives with an evolving, dynamic world in such a way that Christ becomes the centre of history and also its fulfilment; in this regard Teilhard's cosmic Christology was a basis for their investigation and presentation.

On the subject of grace, what emerges from their writings is that grace is about relationship rather than being an entity as such. Grace is the relationship we have with God, in which God offers us as humans a share in the divine life. At all times God takes the initiative, constantly calling us to divine friendship and this is why the relationship is graced, a free gift, and in no way merited as such. Grace starts with God's 'decision' to create and offer humanity a share in the divine life; henceforth humans as part of creation are given an offer to participate in the work of God; creation and human life thus become a share in the divine creativity. We are, in reality, co-creators with God which gives us an innate dignity and is at the same time a call to engage in the ongoing divine creative enterprise. This involves us in answering God's call and responding to the offer of grace in the totality of our human activity. This is a very Teilhardian approach.

God, of course, also endows humans with free will and it is possible for us to fail in our response to the divine call and this is what we call sin. However, grace and sin are not static realities, they are dynamic and played out in an ongoing set of relationships, to God, to others and to the world and its concerns. From this perspective, sin is a failure to answer God's call and the New Testament speaks of sin as "missing the mark", in other words of us not reaching our potential, not responding to God's call in the many relationships of our life. But if God's grace is about relationship then it is possible for this to grow or to wither. Relationships never remain static and sin is a failure to allow our relationship with God to grow. It is not necessarily a question of doing something wrong, 'committing a sin', but can also be failing to do something which will increase our growth in relationship. So rather than speak of sins as acts against God it might be more accurate to speak of sin or sinfulness as a failure to sustain our relationship with God or fulfilling our God-given potential. This is a much more positive way of thinking about grace and sin and makes them more real in our lives. Life, then, is ultimately about our relationship with God and how we respond to the divine call in all that we do in life – our relationship to others in family, society and the world. Sin is a case of not grasping the challenges and opportunities offered to us and hence not growing in our relationship with God.

It is in this larger context that the sacrament of reconciliation has to be understood, for if we fail in our response to God we also fail as members of the human community and weaken its effectiveness as a force for good in the world; thus, we not only say sorry to God for our failures but also to our fellow travellers in church and world, through the agency of the priest who acts as representative of the community. Sin is never solitary but always has a social or community aspect because we are all members of God's people and the human community. Communal celebration of the sacrament of reconciliation makes clear this community aspect of sin but sadly has not been generally embraced within the church, largely I suspect, due to a materialist understanding of sin and grace as things or acts rather than as relationship. What appears to be more important is the rote telling of sins rather than coming together to repair and build relationships. This is really a missed opportunity on the part of the church to make reconciliation a positive, forward looking activity for the whole community and its collective mission to the world.

Looking back at this brief survey of the development of catholic theology leading up to the Second Vatican Council, what stands out is a more open, inclusive view of Christian life and thinking, with an emphasis on people and relationships rather than things or institutions, a dynamic as opposed to a static vision of the world and a church seen as servant of the world and ready to learn from it as well as preach to it. Along with the approach of Teilhard, and no doubt in part due to his influence, there has been a growing awareness of the need for Christians to engage fully with their world and all its concerns and challenges and thus help 'build God's world'.

The Documents of Vatican II

To show how the theological and other developments we have discussed bore fruit in a fuller reception within the Church, I would like to offer a few reflections on the documents of Vatican II, which bring together many of the previous theological approaches. This is not even a summary of Vatican II but rather a pointing up of some of its important teaching. The Council saw itself as primarily pastoral in orientation and not, as with most previous councils, dogmatic; the practicalities of Christian life would be its focus, with a view to supporting and exhorting all members of the church in their responsibilities to bring the message of Christ to the world they live in. The first document to appear was "The Constitution on the Sacred Liturgy", which stressed the central importance of worship in the life of the Church. It begins by declaring that among the main aims of the Council was to invigorate Christian life and make it more suitable to the modern world and thereby increasing the impact of the Church on the world.

As part of this programme of renewal it set out to increase participation of all the faithful in the liturgy and encourages the clergy and those who teach in seminaries to become fully aware of liturgical renewal; it clearly envisaged that without the lead of the clergy any liturgical renewal would flounder. This insight into liturgical education within the Church was significant; unfortunately, the recommendations fell on deaf ears in many parts of the Church, with the result that liturgical renewal was not always understood, and in some cases hardly took place. In reality, many of the clergy were ill prepared for liturgical, or any other, renewal and merely followed the letter of the law in the ensuing development of liturgical change. Not surprisingly, many people had a minimal appreciation of the changes and did not benefit to the full from renewal in the liturgy. Of course, there were exceptions and in many places the liturgical changes that took place were explained fully and as a result a much richer appreciation of the mass and the sacraments was achieved.

One of the most fundamental changes that took place in the liturgy, of course, was the introduction of vernacular languages in place of Latin; for many, this amounted to a sea change while for others it was a most welcome innovation. However, one of the many results of liturgical renewal was a change in attitude to the notion of priesthood, or at least to the role of the priest in the Church. As the liturgy became more intelligible and participative, lay people began to become more involved in public worship and this led to a seeming blurring of the distinction between priest and lay people in relation to their respective roles in the liturgy. The gradual introduction of lay readers and lay ministers of the eucharist was an expression of this; in the missionary countries this was viewed as a necessity, but in the more traditional European and American contexts such changes were more circumspect. This discussion about the relative roles of priesthood and laity continues today, particularly in areas where there are few priests to meet the needs of the faithful. Unfortunately, this issue has been complicated as a result of seeing celibacy as an essential element of priestly life which, in some respects is a separate issue. There has been a fudge on this issue with the introduction of a married diaconate, which is not a complete answer to the problem. The issue of women in the Church and especially in relation to priesthood is an ongoing debate but not at an official level, insofar as Pope John Paul II seemed to imply that this was not an issue open to discussion. On these issues much has yet to be determined.

While the Constitution on the Sacred Liturgy was the first document to emanate from the Council, perhaps the most significant was Lumen Gentium, on the Church. This document more than any other gave a new direction to our understanding of the Church and provided a corrective to previous one-sided views of the nature of the Church.

The Constitution begins with showing how the life of the Church is associated closely with the life of the Trinity, which is the source of life of the Church. The Church is primarily an expression of this divine life, as Body of Christ and inspired by the life of the Holy Spirit. This Spirit was poured out on the disciples at Pentecost and it is from this source that the life of the Church issues, with the mandate to share this patrimony with all humanity – this is the source of the mission of the Church. Thus, the person of Jesus, filled with the Spirit, is the unique source of life of the Church and it is this following of Jesus in faith that forms the basis of the Church and characterizes its nature as a human community with a divine origin. The document goes on to show how the Church, in imitation of its founder, must fulfill its task in poverty and humility and as a form of service to the world.

In speaking of the human constitution of the Church, it is pointed out that all members constitute the People of God by their faith and rebirth in the Spirit; all receive in baptism the call to holiness and consecration to the work of making God's presence a reality in the world. While it notes the difference between the ordained priesthood and the laity it underlines the importance of the shared 'priesthood of Jesus Christ' by all members of the Church, which has its basis in the sacrament of baptism; lay people in the Church are not just followers of the hierarchical priesthood but have their own inherent dignity within the ecclesial dispensation. Prior to the Council, there was a decidedly hierarchical view of the Church, with lay people seen as having a submissive, auxiliary role within the Church rather than as having their own inalienable and specific role to play in the divinely instituted church order.

Following the chapter on the People of God, which emphasizes the fact that all members of the Church share in a common missionary responsibility, further chapters outline the specific roles of the hierarchy and laity within the Church's life and mission and then returns to the Universal Call to Holiness; this is another important and emphatic statement of the need for all members of the Church to recognize the importance of a life of holiness. It is not just priests and religious who have to strive for holiness in their lives; each individual in the Church is called to a life of prayer and holiness and to live out their Christian vocation in the circumstances of their lives, whether it be in family life, at work, in politics or in leisure. This approach is very much in tune with Teilhard's as will become clear in our discussion of his spirituality.

The life and teaching of the Church has always been centred on God's word in the scriptures, though this has not always been visible in many aspects of its life. Due to the predominance of Latin in its language and communication, the scriptures had been almost the preserve of the clergy and of limited accessibility to the faithful. The biblical and liturgical movements of the 20th century gradually made the scriptures more openly available to all. The Constitution on the Liturgy put the scriptures and vernacular language at the heart of its proposals and the *Dogmatic Constitution Dei Verbum* again put the scriptures right at the centre of Christian life with its presentation of the meaning of God's Word and the way in which it speaks to us today. It makes clear the centrality of God's Word in the life of the Church, showing how Christ as the Word of God speaks to us both in the reading of the scriptures and in the celebration of the liturgy which gives sacramental expression to God's message to us and is source of our spiritual life. New translations of the Bible have, of course, added to the availability of the scriptures in our lives and given greater depth and reality to their influence and importance as guides in our spiritual journey. The document also underlines the importance of the biblical narrative in the development of theology and the need to continually confront the scriptures with our modern concerns; theology has to be in continual dialogue with the scriptural witness and not be a separate form of activity. In this respect, the question of tradition as the living expression of God's word has taken on a new importance; tradition is thus seen as a living, developing process and not a dead letter from the past. The increased awareness and use of the scriptures in the liturgy has also made the scriptures live as never before; in addition, the interaction of word and sacrament, word and action, emphasizes the vitality of the Church's life in bringing the reality of God's gift of divine life to realization in today's world.

There has always been an anxiety to "retain the truth", the deposit of faith, an awareness that a gift has been given to the church and that it has to be cherished and preserved. However, this has often been misunderstood or misinterpreted. For many, tradition is regarded as a non-negotiable datum, something that is unchanging and appropriate for every age and therefore cannot be tampered with. This would extend not only to truths of revelation which have their source in the

scriptures but also to theological expression. But this is to misunder-
stand what tradition is. Certainly, the truths expressed in the scriptures
as God's Word are given for all times. However, our grasp and understanding of these truths is always open to development and
enrichment. The Church has to continually reflect on God's Word
and express its meaning for the world in which it finds itself. As history
has progressed, we as humans face different challenges and therefore
have to "search the scriptures" for answers to these challenges. The
gift of the Spirit is an important factor here, as it is the Spirit which
continually reminds us of the life and teaching of Jesus and interprets
for us the meaning of Jesus' message for today. While the Spirit speaks
within the Church, this has to be correctly understood; the Spirit
speaks to all in the Church and not exclusively to the Pope and
Bishops. The "sensus fidelium", the spiritual insight of all the baptized,
is an important element of the guidance of the Spirit within the
Church.

Another distinction that has to be made, of course, is that the formal
teaching of the church, what is usually referred to as the magisterium,
acts as a guide to our understanding; theology and our own personal
understanding of the faith are much more varied in their expression.
Thus, in the Church there may be one faith but there are many ways
of understanding the faith, many theologies. In fact, each individual
has his/her own theology or way of expressing the truths of faith.
Thus, we have to be careful in talking about the unchanging face of
faith. God's word is addressed to all ages and to each individual and
must therefore take different forms or expressions in the circumstances
that it is heard. The great Cardinal Newman was very much aware of
this when he spoke about the development of dogma; he did not
suggest that the revealed truth changes but rather that our understanding of that truth develops. In this respect, God's word expressed
in the scriptures is a rich resource and can never be exhausted. God
still speaks to us in the scriptures today but not in the same way as in
the past. Christians of the first, the third, the tenth, the twentieth
centuries have applied God's word to their lives, in the circumstances
they lived in; we have to do the same in the twenty first century.

So, we see in the teaching of Vatican II a positive and inclusive
Christian vision which must be continually renewed. For many,
Vatican II was seen purely as an end process of earlier developments
and thus the summing up of ideas and practices, a kind of final

synthesis. However, many of those who were present at the Council saw it more of a starting point and a way forward; thus it was a guide to further development, a vison for the future. The danger has always been to treat Vatican II as just a set of documents, written statements, to be read and interpreted, rather than as witnesses to an ongoing spiritual vision, a dynamic process of constant renewal. This inevitably creates tensions regarding the direction and extent of on-going change; it has engendered a good degree of discussion and division within the Church for the past 50 years or so. One of the outcomes of Vatican II was the setting up of Synods of Bishops to take forward the momentum of the Council and return to the world's bishops their leadership in the Church across the world. The synods were supposed to be opportunities for the bishops to discuss important issues and create solutions for their territories along with their brother bishops from across the globe and to supplement or complement the teaching and activity of the Pope. In the event, they became talking shops and the popes gradually decided the agenda and wrote the conclusions and outcomes; this was particularly the case with Pope John Paul II and perhaps to a slightly lesser degree with Pope Benedict. The result has been a diminution of the influence of Vatican II and even a reversal of some of its vision and ideals. There has been a timidity in face of Vatican II's vision of openness and integration and this is expressed in theology returning to a more stringent dogmatism and a wish to return to 'traditional' ideas and practices – a return to the use of Latin in the liturgy and older liturgical practices and more emphasis on 'orthodoxy'. These reversals have found acceptance among those who yearn for a 'comfortable Christianity' where everything is black and white and assured. In a world that is changing so rapidly and where faith is challenged as never before, it is not surprising that many want stability and confidence and to be told what to believe – this is comforting and gives religious faith and practice a feeling of solidity in a sea of change. Pope Benedict encouraged this movement, while at the same time calling for a 'new evangelisation', to improve the Church's promotion of the message of the Gospel. His efforts improved some aspects of the church's life but has done little to make the work of true evangelization more effective. An inward looking renewal has inevitably weakened the Church's outreach to those who have been abandoning active religious practice, especially in Europe but even across the globe. By contrast, Pope Francis has opened up the Church's vision and has clearly signalled the need to abandon our narrow inward-looking approach and to embrace the world in a more positive fashion. For him the Church is servant to the world and has to lose some of its self-importance and regard. However, Pope Francis has faced a degree of opposition from all areas of the Church and is criticized for his openness, his self-effacement and his disdain for the trappings of the Pontificate. He is certainly breaking the mould of papal leadership in the way he says and does things and for many this is a breath of fresh air. What is clear is that Pope Francis recognizes that the Church of today cannot rely on pious platitudes to present its message, it needs action and a courageous option for the poor and the disadvantaged; this is uncomfortable and challenging and requires a complete act of faith and trust in God to carry out. He himself shows by his actions that his faith is not just words; in this he is an example for us to follow. But his way is not easy, it is not assured of success, but it has the mark of the Gospel and Jesus' prescription for bringing in the kingdom. Is the Spirit calling us to a life of comfortable religion, with the comfort of interior faith or to a life of service and challenge where our faith has to be lived in the realities of our world and will cost us? Today, the Church is at a crossroads. Our vision of faith and the spirituality that encapsulates it is being challenged as never before. As Jesus challenged those who heard the parables to make a choice for or against the kingdom, so we are being asked to embrace a faith which is totally inculturated in our worldly concerns and not just in our places of prayer and worship.

In this chapter, I have ranged over the last century and highlighted some of the issues and concerns that have emerged and developed over the years. Faith and spirituality are not isolated things but develop within a mind set and atmosphere formed by the various developments we surveyed and which each of us have to make our own.

In his encyclical *Laudato Si'*, Pope Francis embraced a largely creation-centred theology. In the body of the encyclical he briefly mentions Teilhard de Chardin his Jesuit confrere and advocates his 'cosmic theology' as a useful companion in our creation of a vision of faith for today. We will take his advice in later chapters, where Teilhard's 'spirituality of effort' will be outlined.

What has been significant in the development of theology during the past century is that, despite the presentation of a more biblically based, dynamic and open vision, with a few exceptions it has all been developed within a static world context. This also applies to Pope Francis' world view, which needs to be expanded to take account of our evolutionary world view; Catholic theology is still in the Middle Ages, in a static universe, with God somewhere in the Empyrean sphere and completely separate from the world, unchanging and all powerful. In this context there is a complete cleavage between the order of creation and the order of salvation/redemption. Today we live in a world subject to evolution and on-going change, we have a new understanding of astronomy and our place in the universe and most people take this as the norm. We might therefore ask why in matters of faith we remain in the Middle Ages and fail to live in the present with its scientific understanding and expectations. If the Gospel message is to make any impression on modern humanity it has to live in the same world. This was the fundamental starting point for Teilhard de Chardin. He was a scientist as well as a priest and religious and was acutely aware of the need to be able to communicate his vision of faith to his scientific colleagues. At the same time he recognized the need for any evangelization to speak the same language as the world it was facing. This task was to be his life's work.

Before discussing his offering, we need to consider the implications of our modern understanding of creation and evolution for our faith in God, how a new concept of God is needed. This will be the subject of the next chapter.

CHAPTER FOUR

Where on Earth?
God in an Evolutionary World

In this chapter I want to look at the universe we live in and how our views have changed. It is not necessary to have a deep understanding of astronomy or evolution but it is important to consider the implications of new ways of looking at the world for our understanding of God and of how we relate to God in our daily life.

Teilhard de Chardin, as we saw in Chapter Two, sought a God who was 'as vast and mysterious as the cosmos, immediate and all-embracing as life and linked in some way to our effort as mankind'. This was in contrast to the God envisaged by the theology of his day who was distant and remote, unconnected with our world and our everyday activities and concerns.

The totality of God is, of course, outside our experience and there is a sense in which God is unknown. But he can be known in some way in the depths of our personal being. In the history of thinking about God two aspects have always been seen in apposition – God's otherness, his distance from all earthly reality (transcendence) and God's nearness to us as sustainer of our life (immanence) and there has always been a tension between these two aspects in our efforts to understand the nature of God. Ultimately, God is mystery and we will never have an adequate understanding of the inner being of God. However, there have always been attempts to try and approach an understanding of God and we have turned to both philosophy and religion for some answers and clarification.

In the Old Testament God is seen as both creator and redeemer/deliverer. In Israel's history, God was first experienced as deliverer and the God of the covenant; although Genesis is the first book of the Bible it was not the first to be written and its story of creation was a later reflection by the Jews. In light of their experience of the God of deliverance they looked back at their origins and encountered the creator God. At the same time they reflected on the promises of the creator and their history of rejection of God, the story of mankind played out in the Adam and Eve story. In many ways the God of creation was secondary to the God of salvation, despite the allusions to the beauty and wonder of creation in the psalms and Wisdom literature, and this viewpoint continued up into New Testament times. Although Jesus pointed to the beauty of creation and God's care for all creatures, the emphasis is on salvation brought by Jesus and this is mostly evident in the rest of the New Testament. In St Paul, particularly in his so-called Cosmic texts in Colossians and Ephesians, we have allusion to God's creative power and intentions and these texts became a focus for Teilhard, as we shall see. The prologue to St John's Gospel introduces the Word at the point of creation and this was further developed by some mediaeval theologians such as Blessed John Duns Scotus and the Franciscan tradition as well as Teilhard in the modern era. We shall return to these themes later.

In early Christianity, thinking about God was influenced by Platonic philosophy as well as the biblical tradition. Plato speaks of the cosmos as being made from a model already in the mind of God, so creation imitated the divine archetype and in this respect was viewed as perfect – God's eternity is imitated in the introduction of time and the cosmos (creation/ the universe) becomes an imitation of eternity. Within this context the cosmos is unchanging like God but it is also envisaged as a series of concentric spheres or circles with earth at the centre and then the planets and stars, followed by the Empyrean sphere which leads into the divine spheres which themselves are in an ascending order leading to God; these divine spheres are mentioned by St Paul in the New Testament: angels, archangels, principalities, powers, virtues, dominions, thrones, cherubim and seraphim. These spheres formed a hierarchy of ascending and descending relationships, the lower ones directed by the higher and thus there was a line of increasing importance, power and spirituality from the earth and humans up to God. This was called the Great Chain of Being in which there was a gradual ascent from the material to the spiritual and the aim of the Christian was to move from the material to the spiritual in order to return to God from where they had originated. One consequence of this view of the world was that there was a clear emphasis on the spiritual and a consequent diminution of the importance of the material.

This mediaeval view of the world with the earth at the centre was challenged by Copernicus, Kepler, Galileo and the astronomers of the 16th century onwards; no longer was the earth at the centre of the universe. The Bible had been written in much earlier times and accepted a geocentric universe (the earth at the centre) and an even more primitive picture of the universe. This led to a face-off between science/astronomy and religion due to the importance of biblical truth in the Church's understanding of the world. Eventually there was an acceptance of the new astronomy but the basic view of the universe as developed in the Middle Ages remained; in fact, much of today's Catholic theology retains elements of this world view.

During the 19th century the emergence of evolutionary theory presented yet another challenge to Christianity and its understanding of creation, the world and the place of God. The notion that creation did not take place at one point in time but over a very long period seemed to challenge the notion of a creation by God, it seemed to curtail the power of God. The Church was slow to embrace the challenge apart from individuals such as Teilhard and hence his censure and exile to the nether regions of China where he was to live for more than twenty years. There is still a reluctance to accept an evolutionary understanding of the world and to view God within this context. In a recent theology text for church students, evolution is dismissed in half a page, as a side issue and not really relevant to the discussion of God today, which is a sad reflection on the state of theological discussion in the 21st century.

So, how do we approach this issue in a meaningful way? Perhaps a brief look at some attempts to change the way theology looks at the world might be helpful. In Catholic circles there has been a development of thinking from the 1960s, firstly looking at creation and environmental issues and leading to a fuller treatment of an evolutionary theology. Of course, it is worth mentioning that Teilhard precedes these developments in so many ways and his insights have been extremely influential in recent theological debate.

In 1963 Rachel Carson, an American biologist, wrote a ground-breaking book entitled *The Silent Spring* which was about the dangers of using chemical pesticides; this book is regarded as the beginning of the environmental movement. In 1968 an American academic, Lynn White, accused Christianity of encouraging environmental pollution; he pointed to the Genesis text: "Go forth and multiply and subdue the earth" as the basis for human despoliation of the earth, for humans to lord it over creation as though they were entitled to do what they wished with the earth's resources. This led theologians to scurry to the biblical text and see exactly what it said. The general conclusion was that the notion of subduing the earth was a mis-reading of the Genesis text, which should be understood as humans having responsibility for the earth as God's representative. While this may have satisfied the theologians in rebutting the accusation of Christian responsibility for ecological damage, it soon led to much more positive responses from theologians and a movement towards a theology of creation. In Protestant circles the notion of stewardship of creation became an important theme, while in Catholicism a creation spirituality and a wider ecological theology came on stream. The American Dominican priest, Matthew Fox, wrote his hugely important book, *Original Blessing*, in 1983, which introduced a spirituality which was aligned with environmental and ecological concerns and provided an overview of creation-centred spirituality in the scriptures and Christian history. He showed how there were two narratives from early Christianity right up to the present; one emphasised creation following St Irenaeus and the later Franciscan tradition, while the other stressed redemption following St Augustine and the later Thomistic tradition. He points out that while the redemptive emphasis gained the upper hand in Church thinking up into the present, the creation-centred approach was always present albeit in the background and what was happening was a return to this lost creation-centred theology which was more appropriate in a modern world with its new-found appreciation of creation as the primary entry into our understanding of God.

In 1988, the American Passionist Fr Thomas Berry published *The Dream of the Earth*, which contained a range of essays on the theme of creation; for Berry creation is 'the primary revelation of the divine'. Berry was an expert on Chinese Buddhism and had taught world religions for many years; his contact with Chinese thinking had engendered an interest in the relationship between religion and the natural world and a reading of Teilhard de Chardin's *The Human Phenomenon* led to him setting up the Riverdale Centre for Religious Research in New York and a life-long devotion to an ecological Christian spirituality. In *The Dream of the Earth* he spoke of the Story of the Earth as the most important feature of our Christian understanding of God and the world. He points out that the work of creation and its history reveals God's activity as much as does the scriptures. In this he was repeating St Bonaventure's notion of the Two Books of Revelation: in creation and the Bible. Along with the scientist Brian Swimme he wrote about our relationship with the universe, of how we are born in the stars and are part of the story of the universe. This takes us to the heart of an understanding of how evolution is God's way of creating and we need to unpack this a little further in order to appreciate its significance.

Evolutionary thinking leads us to see creation not as a once-for-all event but as an ongoing activity; creation is taking place all the time. Within this context God continues to create and is at the heart of this on-going creative process. Evolution means that creation is not so much an event as a process, a dynamic activity. This contrasts with the more traditional static view of the world in which creation starts the ball rolling and then there is an unchangeable state of being over which God, as it were, stands guard from a distant shore. This view has the effect of making God feel remote and disconnected from us and the world. In an evolutionary world, God is still involved in the creative process and is at the very heart of the world. God is within creation as its motive energy. This accentuates God's immanence over God's transcendence; God is the silent and unseen force of creation. But this way of understanding creation implies some important notions about our relationship to God which has implications for God and for ourselves. If we can talk of God deciding to create in an evolutionary fashion, this involves a process of change and implies an unfinished universe at any one time; thus, creation is yet to be completed and has not yet reached fulfilment. God in this respect does not create a perfect universe but a universe on the journey to perfection. If we factor in ourselves as elements of creation, God has given us the gift of freedom and this leaves the future open to some extent. In other words, we have an effect on the outcome of the creative venture and God depends on us as to the outcome of creation. This is a conundrum; on the one hand we have God's plan of creation which emanates from the perfect Being, on the other hand we have the freedom to affect the outcome insofar as we have an influence on the creative process. This is difficult to understand and we have to put it into the wider context of God's providence which at the same time preserves God's control over the divine plan for creation but also leaves human freedom intact. This has always been part of theological thinking and tries to understand the relationship between our activity in freedom and the will of God, the eternal plan of God. Inevitably we are faced with a mystery and can only hold to both sides of the equation: God's overarching will and our freedom within God's plan.

Teilhard was often accused of being too optimistic over the outcome of the evolutionary process, believing that God's love would ultimately bring the process to a positive fulfilment despite the influence of human failure and sin. What Teilhard firmly believed was that we humans are co-creators with God and we are crucial in God's plan of bringing creation to a positive conclusion. This gives us an awesome privilege but an equally tremendous responsibility to cooperate with God in the divine plan to share the divine life with humanity. However, there is another implication in this way of looking at things which concerns the world, the universe itself. If God has created such an infinite universe, which science and astronomy is continually revealing to us in ever greater clarity and immediacy, then the universe itself has an innate meaning. We have to ask whether God would create such an immense universe merely to make a place for us as humans to prove ourselves for heaven. When we consider that the universe is so immense and intricate to an extent we can scarcely take in and that the earth and ourselves represent such a truly minute element within this universe, we have to wonder whether there must be a meaning in and a future for the universe as part of God's plan. Science tells us that the universe is unlikely to be eternal and will come to an end at some point in the future but what this future might look like is not known. Some would suggest that the universe is gradually shrinking and is on a downward course towards extinction, while some have suggested that we live in an expanding universe. So the future is an open question.

If we take even a glimpse of the universe as revealed by science and astronomy we are faced with a beautiful universe of almost unimaginable size and expanse; the expanse of the universe is truly mind-boggling and we can but admire the work of the creator. But at the same time this universe is subject to change and movement which can be both violent and uncertain and we are at the mercy of the forces of the universe. What is truly fantastic to consider is how utterly small the earth is in the span of the universe and how the very existence of the earth is a miracle because the likelihood of the conditions for life on earth becoming a reality were infinitesimally small. The earth is unique in this respect and, for many, this very unlikelihood of life in the universe is itself an indication of a divine presence in the design of creation.

Teilhard offers some thoughts on the future of the evolutionary journey and we will meet them later. Here we need to complete our discussion of evolutionary creation with a few thoughts on our own part in the evolutionary story. If we take evolutionary theory seriously then we realise that we are products of evolution. We are the result of an evolutionary process which begins in the early history of the universe, the Big Bang, the emergence of the cosmic elements, the formation of planets and other stellar bodies (we are born in the stars!). In describing the evolutionary process Teilhard uses the French word *gènese* which can mean beginning (as in the Book of Genesis) but Teilhard uses it as meaning growth or development, for him it points to a developmental process, as becomes clear when we consider the stages of evolution as he describes it.

The first phase of evolutionary history Teilhard calls cosmogenesis – the development of the cosmos/ universe.

The second phase, which he calls biogenesis, sees the beginnings of the requirements for life – an atmosphere and conditions for life, from single cell organisms to plants, fish, birds and animals.

This is followed by anthropogenesis – the emergence of human beings who have self-consciousness and are able to appreciate their environment and become the self-consciousness of creation itself. Humanity is in some respects the pinnacle of the creative process and therefore has an important role in leading the process to fulfilment. What this signals is that we cannot separate ourselves from the rest of creation, the whole universe, and there is an immediate and ineluctable relationship between ourselves and our earthly environment; in thinking about our relationship to God it is defined by the unbroken line which links the whole creative process in which we emerge from God within the birth of the universe. There is no separation of creation and redemption – they both belong together as an expression of the divine desire to share the divine life as an expression of love and inclusion. Thus a creation-centred theology encapsulates the realities of the divine creative plan.

Returning to the phases of evolution, Teilhard adds two further stages:

1. Noogenesis, the development of a thinking layer over the earth, which will be capable of drawing things together and working as a focus of love to energise the progress of evolution. This involves the development of mind or human consciousness as a directive force within the process of history on earth. This gives humanity a crucial role in the progress of evolution insofar as human beings are the self-consciousness of the universe, they are able to appreciate and influence the evolutionary process. This is an awesome responsibility. Teilhard would have seen the emergence of computers, the world-wide web and artificial intelligence as part of the development of the noosphere.

2. Christogenesis – the gradual influence of Christ in the world, bringing it to completion in God. This will include the Incarnation of God in the world – Christ Jesus, his life, death and resurrection, the sending of the Spirit as the presence of God's love at the heart of creation history leading to its fulfilment at the end of time, the Second Coming of Christ or Parousia.

I will return to these two stages when I discuss Teilhard's ideas in more detail in Chapter Seven.

What all this discussion of evolution means is that we are part of the universe, we belong to it, it is part of our story too; it is not just where we have been planted by God to listen to the divine call, independent of our environment. No, the world is God's world within which we meet the divine summons and the divine call of love. Thus, the world has meaning in God's plan and has its own destiny along with ours. This also means that we have a responsibility for the world, as its self-consciousness, a God-given role in bringing the divine creative venture to fulfilment. If God's creative purpose is to be fulfilled God needs us. Yes, God needs us, the all-powerful creator-God is dependent on us. This seems to limit the power of the All-powerful God in a way that destroys the very notion of God as traditionally understood. However, there is a line of thinking called process theology which believes that in deciding to share the divine life outside the Godhead in creation, God allows creatures a freedom to accept or refuse this offer of a share in divine life. This opens the possibility of divine generosity being compromised and in a way God 'suffers' (this is referred to as the passibility of God), God lowers the divine ultimate power in an act of extreme love. This reminds us of the passage in Philippians 2,5–7 referring to Christ: "His state was divine, yet he did not cling to his equality with God but emptied himself to assume the condition of a slave."

Is this an intimation of a God who expresses ultimate love in opening divine initiative to human refusal? This is a difficult question but certainly asks us to reflect deeply on what a God of love might mean.

Returning to the whole evolutionary process and our involvement in it, we come to a realisation of our responsibility for the whole of creation. This is not just about being interested in or aware of the environment, doing our bit for recycling, although it includes these; it means that our relationship with God has to be lived out in the daily activities of our life, in the responsibilities and relationships we have, in a concern for all those who are in need. Our relationship to and response to the call of God will be determined to the extent we change God's world for the better and give ourselves fully to the building of God's world. This is how we will respond to Jesus' call to build the kingdom of God. The kingdom is not in the future but here on earth and the values of this kingdom are contained in the life and message of Jesus. Our response to his call will require our complete dedication and will cost in terms of sacrifice and suffering. The sufferings of Jesus symbolise and encapsulate the effort required to build God's world.

So, evolution is not a side show, just a fanciful theory, but is at the very heart of our Christian life and task. It also implies a life of change, movement and dynamism in all aspects of our life. This will be further investigated in the next chapter. At the end of the day, we are involved in cooperating with God in the whole creative venture, from the creation of the universe right down to the progress of life on earth and the making of a human society that reflects the very values of God. We are, in other words, building God's world – this is the bottom line. Every aspect of creation is linked in an unbroken skein of divine activity.

CHAPTER FIVE

All Change
Living in a Dynamic World

Evolution is more than just a theory about the universe and human origins as revealed in scientific explanation, it represents the character of change which underlies the whole of reality. Life, in evolutionary terms, is dynamic and this is no less the case with Christian life and spirituality. This dynamism and subjection to continual change is a basic law of living and is evident in all aspects of our life, but here I want to concentrate specifically on aspects of Christian life within an evolutionary world. In order to cover the various areas, I will look at the following topics: (a) the underlying dynamic of Christian life; (b) creation centred spirituality and the ecological imperative; and (c) the nature of our life in the Church and the character of the kingdom of God as the essential inspiration for our mission as Christians. As we shall see, in this perspective we as humans and the world around us are so intimately connected that they cannot be separated, we share a common destiny: the future of the world and our future go together.

The Underlying Dynamic of Christian Life

The dynamic of Christian life begins in the life of God and the trinitarian movement of love, as a result of which we are offered a share in the divine life. This is expressed in the divine will to create and allow the inner love of God to become a reality outside the divine life; at the same time, this creative intention includes the presence of the divine in creation in a special way in order to ensure that creatures are able to meet and appreciate the love of God in the creative initiative. This includes the intention to make the Word of creation a real presence in the world in such a way that it will make the loving intentions of God intelligible and enable all creation to respond to the offer of God's love. While God is always present in creation in a hidden way, acting as its motive energy, Christ enters the world to make God present among us in a vivid and accessible fashion, to show us the way to respond to God's love and represent the energy and love of God in the ongoing creation and bring it to fulfilment. Knowing that creatures will be imperfect and subject to a process of growth toward perfection, Christ will also represent the love and mercy of God towards all creatures in their journey towards perfection. The resurrection of Christ will express the life-giving power of God in a dramatic and final way; this power of the Risen Christ will be exercised throughout time by the presence of the Spirit. At the same time, the creative venture of God centred on Christ will reach its fulfilment in the final bringing-together of God's creative plan in the Parousia, the Second Coming of Christ at the end of time when the Pleroma (fulness) of God will be revealed and creation will reach its conclusion.

This whole process is a dynamic movement in which creation begins in the life of the Trinity, and it is Christ-centred insofar as the completion of creation is coterminous with the completion of Christ. Christ is willed as the completion of creation from the very outset; he doesn't come into the world as a result of sin and would have become incarnate in any circumstance, as taught by Blessed John Duns Scotus in the 14th century. This underpins the notion of Christ as the meaning of creation: as St Paul reminds us, "In him all things hold together". The presence of God in creation is summed up in the Body of Christ, which brings together all of creation and particularly human creation. The Church as Body of Christ is a sacramental expression and anticipation of this Body but must look to the incorporation of all things in Christ so that ultimately the whole of creation is the real Body of Christ. Within this context, Christ's incarnation, life, message, death and resurrection are all part of one movement from the initial creative intention of God to its completion at the end of history. There is no separation of creation and salvation/redemption, but one integrated plan of God in which the entire creation and not just humans are part of the design of God. As humans we are given the gift and privilege but also the awesome responsibility of being co-creators with God and so our spiritual destiny is one with our human destiny. Spiritual fulfilment can only be accomplished through complete dedication to bringing God's creation to fulfilment.

The question of the outcome of creation, the outcome of evolution, is one that has yet to be determined in any detail. We face an open future and have to work with our fellow humans to carve out that future. Although the future is ultimately in the hands of God, we are tasked with doing all we can to discern God's design and purpose into the future. This can only be achieved by cooperation with all our human neighbours; the Church has to reach out to and embrace all of humanity in order to bring creation to a positive conclusion. Pope Francis has repeatedly urged us to get involved in the world and its needs for the future. He recognises that this will demand dedication and sacrifice; he is nothing if not a realist and knows that this world is full of temptations and dead ends as well as beautiful attractions and opportunities. Evolution is a battle and a continual struggle, with competing demands for reaching into the future. This appears as the basic law of all evolutionary development, in the natural world with disasters and set-backs (acts of God !!), in the vast and varied vagaries of the animal world and of course in human history and social existence. In our contribution to evolutionary history and progress we need to use all our God-given human gifts of enquiry and invention as well as our human values of honesty, persistence and cooperation. We also need to invoke the help, assistance and inspiration of God and live the values of the kingdom presented by Jesus as the way of God to live our lives. The example of Jesus is of paramount importance and especially his sacrifice in facing the challenges of life; the suffering and complete dedication of Jesus to the will of the Father is a perfect example for us in our dedication to the work of 'building God's world', his sacrifice on the cross represents the effort of humanity in the work of bringing evolution to fulfilment.

In our evolutionary world we experience change at every turn. If we consider the past century of our history it is clear that as evolution continues on its forward journey the speed of change increases with almost frightening regularity. Teilhard speaks of the path of evolution as similar to the shape of a cone; as we reach the apex of the cone it becomes smaller and the path tightens and becomes more restrictive. The further along the evolutionary journey we travel the more daunting the task becomes. This presents many challenges and can be both exhilarating and forbidding, requiring decisions on many levels, including social, economic and moral. We become aware that as humans we can influence the shape of the future and the outcome of evolution. As Christians we have an important contribution to make in creating the shape of the future and this is an awesome task, a responsibility given to us as co-creators in the divine plan for creation. It will make demands on our time, our effort and our involvement in the life of our world, be it in building our own family or local community, working for the wider society or taking an interest in and responding to specific needs that arise in the world at large. In a memorable phrase Pope Francis speaks about caring for 'our common home' which implies that in all this work we must work with all our human neighbours in an open and cooperative fashion and continually 'read the signs of the times' to discern the call of God in the circumstances of our life. This requires a commitment to 'building God's world' in all the circumstances of our life, the hum drum and normal as well as the extraordinary and times of emergency. There is not an area of life that does not become a part of this effort.

Creation Centred Spirituality and Ecological Responsibility

God's world in which we live encompasses everything, including the natural world in all its various forms, the animal world and human society in all its complexity. When Pope Francis talks about caring for our common home he does not restrict this to human life and its concerns but also includes the whole of the natural world. There has been a tendency to see care for the natural world and interest in the environment as optional extras and almost side issues; however, in recent years there has been much more emphasis on the importance of nature and the wider creation as the responsibility of everyone. It has taken more time for this thinking to percolate down to spirituality and Christian living. There has been a failure to view creation as an integrated whole, encompassing the human and non-human world, along with an almost exclusive emphasis on human relationships and our relationship with God in prayer as the focus for spiritual life, with little reference to our responsibilities as stewards of creation. There is a need to return to an integrated vision in which all are seen equally as part of God's creation and thus awaiting final fulfilment in God's final creative act. Our destiny as humans is inextricably linked to the future of creation as a whole, the entire universe.

The world of creation in all its variety reveals the amazing originality and newness of God and must be cherished as such and at the same time accepted as the divine project to be brought to completion. Thomas Berry in his many writings speaks of the earth as being the primary revelation of the divine and the place where God and humans meet in communion. He reminds us that we are the self-consciousness of the universe and as such must try to bring about the integration of the inner spiritual reality and the outer physical form in an integrated vision. In one of his essays Berry refers to St Thomas Aquinas who said that the variety of created forms was necessary to express the beauty of God, as any one element was insufficient to do this. Berry goes on to say that our own creativity throughout history expresses the many aspects of the divine creativity; but he also points out that the universe has both a violent and a harmonious aspect but that it is always creative. This insight is a constant reminder to us that in our human experience, at all levels and in all its various aspects, we are faced with an unfinished universe, a work in progress, which inevitably reflects the brokenness and incomplete character of the world we live in. This is the challenge that is set before us. We are all aware of the sickness and suffering, the human brokenness and inefficiency, which marks our humanity and which can lead to despondency and despair in the face of the task before us. However, if we see these as expressions of the work of redeeming the universe and as part of the divine healing process leading to eventual glory and fulfilment, then we will be able to welcome them in a spirit of trust and confidence in the love of God and the hope of final success. The life of Jesus is a very clear example of this attitude; he gave himself to the work of the Father even when it seemed to be hopeless and meaningless and his journey through suffering and death to resurrection provides a singular example of the faith and trust in God which is required in our own journey through evolutionary history and in our daily lives.

In practical terms, our commitment to the work of bringing creation to its fulfilment has to include a number of personal and communal responses. Care for the environment is an essential element of our commitment and is not an optional extra. We can get involved in all sorts of worldly activities and concerns in order to show our commitment to create a society of equality and concern for all but this awareness of the needs of the world must extend to concern for the world about us, the natural environment. The resources of the earth are our life-line and enable us to continue in existence but they are also limited and have to be shared among all peoples across the globe; thus it is a case of a necessity for continued life and an issue of sharing resources – but not just self-preservation but also justice. This is a problem for everyone and not just for the dreamy-eyed environmental campaigners. We are talking here about our common concern for the earth as Pope Francis reminds us. We are living in a world of inequality and injustice which does not reflect the community of divine love which we are called to implement. We need to rethink our life-styles and be part of a movement to introduce the values of the kingdom as outlined by Jesus in his parables and in the Sermon on the Mount; only thus will there be a future leading to equality for all and a sustainable existence into the future. Jesus' teaching was in many respects simple but it was also revolutionary and overturned normal expectations; we only have to reflect on the topsy-turvy logic of the parables and the radical call for metanoia – repentance, or complete change of attitude and way of life – to realise how transforming the values of the kingdom were meant to be.

In our care for the environment we become aware of the interconnectedness of all things, that each and every element has its own part to play in the complicated web of relationships which lie at the heart of our life on earth. Plants, insects, animals – what we refer to as the natural environment – are all part of an intricate system of life; there are micro and macro life systems of which we are not always fully aware. If we remove species or their means of subsistence, their habitats, we set in motion a series of repercussions which can have devastating effects for the whole of the environment including human society. We only have to look at what has happened as a result of over-farming, the removal of rain forests and other human interventions in the environment to realise the implications of such activities for the entire human community and the future of earth. As humans, we have a responsibility to manage the environment in a way that respects the rights of all to continued existence; as the leading force in the march of evolution we have a lot of crucial decisions to make about the shape of the future and in this work we have to collaborate with all those who are involved in the management of resources and systems. There are no ready-made solutions, but our Christian insights will be of crucial importance in ensuring that the values of equality, love and justice characterise the decisions and actions undertaken. We need to keep in mind the importance of earth systems for human life, the rights of the non-human world (animals and other living creatures and their habitats) which are difficult to determine in many situations, and the underlying interrelationships which form the basis for all life. The scientist James Lovelock introduced the notion of Gaia, the universe as a self-regulating entity; this envisaged the universe as a kind of living being which reacts to its environment in a way that living beings do. In this respect the earth has ways of reacting to healing its systems, which have often been harmed by unthinking or selfish human activity. This is a reminder of our need to relate to our environment in a meaningful way and understand its needs. Maybe we forget our dependence on the earth, our mother, from whom we receive all that is necessary for our life, and our need to listen to its requirements as well as its influence on us, often in hidden ways. The Coronavirus pandemic is a reminder that the natural world in its various embodiments has an influence on us and can respond to our negative and harmful actions towards it. There is a real reciprocity between the earth and ourselves which we need to become more aware of and understand as we continue to use the produce of the earth in a forgetful and often wasteful fashion.

On a personal basis, we need to look at our own life-style and choices in all areas of our life, consider the use we make of our environment in the local area and of how we use our own resources. As members of Western society we may need to re-evaluate our standard of living in the light of the evident inequality in world-wide society and the rising numbers of those in poverty, inequality and lack of representation in their societies.

Finally, we need to consider all the above issues as both human and spiritual concerns; our concern should not be so much to 'save our soul' but rather to save God's world of which we are a crucial element in that its future is in our hands along with God.

Life in the Church and Living the Values of the Kingdom

Our life as Christians is lived within the community of the Church which should anticipate in its life and structures the coming of the kingdom and look forward to the completion of God's creative purpose. This requires that the Church offer a living vision within a contemporary setting which can inspire and support God's people to incarnate this vision in their personal and social setting. Essential to this ecclesial vision is its creation-centredness and cosmic character and an acknowledgement of our evolutionary context. If we look at the theological offering in the Church today it is still largely framed within a static world vision and pays too little attention to the contemporary, evolutionary context. We still hear talk about original sin, Adam and Eve as real people, the ability to obtain indulgences, a great deal about sin and repentance and God's mercy for sinners; most liturgical and communal celebrations necessitate an initial act of repentance and ask for forgiveness for sin and in welcoming the catechumens to baptism they are first asked if they deny Satan and his wiles rather than whether they have made a choice for God. All these examples point to a negative approach to faith and in many ways cast God in the role of accuser rather than as a God of love who wishes to engage with us in a positive and loving embrace. Do we really believe in a God of love? Created in an unfinished universe we are not perfect and God understands this and having made us imperfect wishes to lead us to perfection. St Irenaeus understood this perfectly when he speaks of us being made in the image of God and needing to grow into the likeness of God. This presents a much more positive view of our relationship to God and the developmental nature of our growing closer to God. While we have to be aware of and acknowledge our weaknesses, our failure to respond to God's call in the various aspects of our life and our need to grow closer to God, the insistent reminder of sinfulness both disincentivizes those who are seeking God in their lives and devalues the love and mercy of God. In terms of evangelism, a Gospel message of love and openness is much more attractive to seekers than one which emphasises our wretchedness and incapacity. The Gospel, the Good News, should inspire and provide an impetus for positive action and give human activity added purpose and meaning. Earlier I alluded to the notion of grace as relationship and sin as failure to respond to God's love and this dynamic view of our relationship to God should find a greater presence in our theology and preaching. There has always been great importance to confession, or reconciliation as it should be termed, but this has been perhaps the most neglected sacrament as far as renewal is concerned. The very term reconciliation gives a much more positive meaning to the sacrament and should be used in preference to confession which has a more accusatory feeling about it. The other issue is about the way in which sin is considered in a solitary or individual fashion rather than as part of our common journey in faith. Sin is not just about our personal relationship to God, it is also about our relationships to our fellow humans and brothers and sisters in faith. Sin affects our ability to contribute to our common responsibilities; if it is viewed purely as a failure in our relationship with God in the secret of our heart, it suggests that all the other relationships we have are of lesser import or even of no significance. Jesus was very clear about the two-fold nature of love, of God and neighbour. He even tells us that if we do not love our neighbour then we cannot love God either. So, the sacrament of reconciliation has to reflect the social nature of sin and this should be expressed in some form of communal celebration, where everyone present can come to an awareness of their responsibilities to each other and also of their common weakness and need of God's forgiveness. Sadly, the use of a common celebration has been consigned to the dust bin of liturgical usage in favour of individual 'confession' which requires the enumeration of sins as a requirement for absolution rather than a meaningful reflection by all members of the community on the need for forgiveness in the various aspects of our life in which we fail to express the values of the Gospel in a meaningful way. A communal reflection followed by a communal act of forgiveness and absolution, in which the penitents are treated as adults and left to their conscience in admitting their personal sin and taking responsibility for their consequent actions would be a more fitting, adult and meaningful celebration of the sacrament. There is no reason why catechesis on communal reconciliation could not prepare everyone in the community for meaningful, genuine and more fruitful use of the sacrament, Where are our bishops in giving the lead here? It would appear they are still wedded to an outdated and gradually diminishing sacramental form. Is it surprising that very few actually use the sacrament.

The eucharist has always been at the centre of our worship and is the source and inspiration of all our efforts as co-creators in the on-going work of divine creation. This needs to be further underlined and strengthened in order to make the eucharist of greater moment and meaning in Christian living. There has been a tendency to view the eucharist as merely a point of receiving – the presence of the Lord and communion on a personal basis. This is a rather restrictive and static way of thinking of the eucharist for essentially it is a dynamic action and the source and impetus for mission. When we gather to celebrate the eucharist the gathering is itself an important feature for it heralds the witness of the Christian community to the message of Jesus and its intention to share its gift with others, taking the message to the world at large in obedience to Jesus' command after his resurrection. The eucharist has a missionary intention at its very heart and is not an occasion to receive Jesus as personal gift but rather as the Risen Presence in the world to bring about its salvation. The Risen Christ who comes to us in the eucharist becomes the energising presence of God in the world; Christ appears under the forms of bread and wine, symbolising the realities of the created world. Through reception of Christ as part of the eucharistic celebration, we become part of Christ and his active presence at the heart of creation and make this presence a reality in our daily lives, consecrating ourselves to the work of Christ and the formation of his Body, the mystical and cosmic Body of Christ. Thus the eucharist is at the heart of evolutionary dynamism, it is an essentially missionary moment and the source of all we do as Christians in the world. This gives the Sunday mass its character of joy in the Risen Christ, its binding together the whole community for its primary purpose – to witness to Christ in the world. It is the starting point for mission and in receiving Christ in communion we are energised as a community and have to take this enthusiasm and energy into the rest of our week. The way in which we celebrate the eucharist should reflect its missionary character by emphasising the element of coming together as community, linking the Word of God and its message in the liturgy of the Word to the fulfilment of the word in the presence and action of Christ. While Sunday eucharist is the central action of the community even daily mass should be seen in the same way and not merely as a personal, warm and intimate encounter with Christ – every eucharist is a call to mission and cannot be separated from our commitment to mission. This links to the notion of church as servant, the fact that the church is not for itself but for the world in which it lives; this is the Church viewed as primarily the people of God, the community of salvation and not just the Church as organisation and hierarchical institution which should act as the enabler of the community in its work of mission. The eucharistic liturgy, of course, has its own character and ethos— its own language, symbolism and actions which belong to a long tradition of liturgical presence — but this should not bind the community to the past but always resonate with changing communities so that the liturgy remains an active inspiration rather than an archaic ritual which stays at the level of passive performance. A fine balance has to be effected between preserving liturgical purity and authenticity and at the same time making it an inspiration to modern sensibilities. Essential to this process is a thorough catechesis on worship, language and music and the ethos of liturgical participation which is the ultimate intention.

We can summarise the above reflections as a need to integrate all our Christian, spiritual activity in a dynamic way, embracing the human and the non-human world as equally important elements of the world to be brought to perfection in God's creative enterprise. Furthermore, our Christian worship, prayer and spiritual activity must be related to the fundamental activity of 'building God's world' and not separated from our human life and social responsibilities. The whole gamut of human activity, care for the natural environment and spiritual concerns and activity must form one seamless garment rather than independent pieces of apparel.

In the following chapters I will attempt to put some flesh onto the bones of an integrated spirituality by looking at the spiritual thinking of Teilhard de Chardin, who made it his life's work to make the spiritual quest and the consecration of the created world a unified project.

CHAPTER SIX

The Christian Vision of Teilhard de Chardin

Who was Pierre Teilhard de Chardin?

I do not propose to write a biography here but merely provide some basic information which may help the reader to appreciate the context within which Teilhard lived and thought and understand his basic concerns and the extent to which his writing still has much to offer us sixty years after his death.

Pierre Teilhard de Chardin, usually referred to as simply Teilhard, was born in the Auvergne region of France in 1881, one of eleven children. His father inspired Pierre's love of nature and the sciences, while his mother was a great influence on his religious outlook. As a young man he was attracted to the life of a priest but also wanted to follow a scientific career. He often speaks, in this regard, of his "two loves", God and the world. After much inner turmoil he took the advice of one of his Jesuit teachers to combine a scientific and priestly career as a Jesuit. He entered the Society of Jesus and began his philosophical studies in Jersey, followed by a short period teaching science to students at a Jesuit school in Cairo. He returned to study at the theologate in Hastings, England and then moved to Paris to begin his scientific studies which would lead to a Doctorate in Palaeontology. However, World War One intervened and he enlisted as a stretcher bearer, seeing service at the Front at Verdun and other places and was later honoured for his bravery in retrieving his fellow soldiers from the dangers of the battlefield. Surprisingly, it was at this time that he wrote his first essays, in between periods of active engagement with the enemy. One of his first essays was "Cosmic Life", in which he reflected on the place of humanity in the world; essentially, he sees humanity as inextricably bound up with the future of the world and spoke of humans as "cosmic beings", due to their shared destiny with the world/cosmos. THIS IS THE BASIS FOR HIS 'COSMIC CHRISTIANITY'.

After the war he returned to complete his studies and was destined for a great academic career in palaeontology and geology but after a short visit to China he returned to Paris and wrote a short essay on how original sin might be envisioned within an evolutionary world-view. Although the essay was not written with a view to publication, it was surreptitiously taken from his room and eventually landed in the hands of over zaelous religious superiors and Church censors. As a result he was "exiled" to China, considered to be dangerous in his theological views. He remained in China until the end of the Second World War and during his time there he undertook a large number of studies and investigations in palaeontology and geology. He was involved in the discovery of the famous "Peking Man" fossils in 1927 and other important finds. At the same time, he continued to write on religious themes and finished his book of spirituality, *Le Milieu Divin* in 1927 and his great survey of cosmic and human history *Le Phenomene Humain* (1941) (Originally translated as *The Phenomenon of Man* but in a later translation as *The Human Phenomenon*). Unfortunately, Teilhard was refused permission to publish any of his religious writings and his works were only published after his death, despite his numerous attempts to convince his Jesuit Superiors and the Roman authorities of his orthodoxy. However, he managed to distribute copies of his essays to a small group of friends and close associates so that his thinking had a limited exposure but he did not have the opportunity to share his ideas openly, which might have enabled his thinking to develop and mature to a greater extent.

From 1946 until his death on Easter Sunday 1955 he lived for the most part in New York, although he made many visits to France, Britain and South Africa on study tours and scientific projects.

As a scientist, Teilhard was extremely aware of the need to speak to those who were not religious or Christian in ways that they could understand and it was this experience that led him to frame Christian thinking in new and novel ways. He was a deeply committed Christian, with a tremendous depth of vision and wanted to share his vision with others. He often spoke of SEEING as central to his thinking and he wanted to share with others how he saw God and the world.

As a theology student in Hastings, he was fortunate to be taught by some brilliant New Testament scholars such a Ferdinand Prat and

Leonce de Grandmaison and it was at this time that he read the Epistles of St Paul and was captivated by the cosmic vision presented by especially Colossians and Ephesians. These insights opened up a vision of the Cosmic Christ which was to become a central pole of his thinking. What he saw in these writings was a Christ who was not just a redeemer but the consummation of God's creative enterprise, the fulfilment of God's plan from the beginning. Everything was directed to Christ and the plan of God would come to fruition and completion when Christ returned at the end of time, the Parousia, as the Pleroma or fullness of God. The centrality of the Cosmic Christ in Teilhard's writing leads to a vision of Christian life as a form of co-creation with Christ, leading the world to its completion in God; what this implies is that ALL human activity has salvific significance, everything we do cooperates in God's work of continuing creation. It is this central insight that underlies all Teilhard's thinking, his spiritual vision; he speaks of "building God's world" as the prime motivation of faith and the basis for a truly Christian humanism. In this respect there is no separation of Christian life/spirituality and our worldly activities, for the aim of Christian life and faith is to make God's presence in the world a reality.

For Teilhard, God's creation of the universe was not a whim but a positive creative impulse; thus, creation has meaning in itself because it is an expression of God's plan which includes humanity. Both the universe and humanity together form part of God's gift of self and should be viewed as God's free gift. Creation is God's gift and is not just an accompaniment to the creation of humanity, merely a place for humans to work out their salvation as so often portrayed in traditional Christian thinking. He considered that if created reality is the work of God then it is not incidental or merely a background to the drama of human salvation but has intrinsic meaning and value and should be accepted as such by us.

The refusal of publication of his writings was a continual source of frustration and sadness for Teilhard and he suffered periods of depression as a result. Nevertheless, he continued to write and to disseminate his ideas to a small circle of friends and fellow Jesuits, including Henri de Lubac who became an advocate for Teilhard and wrote several books of exposition and clarification of Teilhard's views. De Lubac, of course, had himself been under suspicion in Rome but was later given the seal of approval and was made a Cardinal before he died; he understood Teilhard's situation very clearly from his own experience.

Towards the end of his life Teilhard wrote two very important essays which sum up his life's work. In "The Heart of Matter", written in 1950, he tried to set out the progress of his thinking, from his years in the trenches of the First World War to his later years in America and Europe and describes it as a 'sort of biography'. What he finds there is that his thinking did not substantially change but merely developed along a unified vision. This is complemented by the central theme of his last major essay, "The Christic", written in 1955, just a month before his death. Here he shows how the Cosmic Christ is at the very centre of his thinking and is his signature theological contribution to modern Christian thinking. It is interesting how, looking back at his life and thinking, Teilhard recognises the continuity of his work from the early days during the trenches to his later years as a scientific researcher in New York.

Teilhard died on Easter Sunday 1955 following a massive heart attack; he had once said that he would like to die on the feast of the Risen Christ and he was given his wish! Sadly, he died a largely unknown man and was buried alongside his confreres in a Jesuit cemetery near the Hudson river outside New York which is now within the grounds of a hotel and his grave is largely anonymous. In many respects this highlights Teilhard's destiny within the Catholic Church, to be a prophet – unheard and even scorned in his own country!!

Teilhard and his Mission

As early as 1919 Teilhard set out his stall, so to speak, in an essay entitled: Note on the Presentation of the Gospel in a New Age. This essay is one of the most perceptive and prescient of his writings and could easily have been written today as a prescription for the needs of the Church and its message to our modern world. Despite its date, it is as fresh today as it was when he first penned it. In many respects, this essay sets out for the first time his life project: to make Christian life pertinent to the modern world and to show that not only is Christianity compatible with a thoroughly modern way of life but is also essential to the success of the evolutionary movement which underlies the progress of the world we live in. He notes how the world, the universe, has become humanity's God and how

Christianity and its concerns have been pushed to the margins of human consideration. Two things have to change in order to make Christianity a driving force in the world and meaningful to individuals: a re-appraisal of the Christian task and a new understanding of the reality of God. He writes:

"The God for whom our century is waiting must be:
1. As VAST and mysterious as the Cosmos
2. As IMMEDIATE and all-embracing as Life
3. As LINKED (in some way) to our effort as Mankind.
A God who made the World less mysterious, or smaller, or less important to us, than our heart and reason show it to be, that God – less beautiful than the God we await – will never be He to whom the Earth kneels." (HM/NPG 212)

These words underline his conviction that God is not a spectator, standing outside the course of cosmic and human history but rather is at the centre, within history, animating and energising its progress; central to this picture of God is the figure of Jesus Christ who is the ultimate presence of God in history, through whom history finds its meaning and its ultimate fulfilment. At the same time, humanity shares in God's creativity which gives all human activity its ultimate importance; in the same way, humanity is linked essentially to the destiny of the cosmos, the universe, and for this reason Teilhard speaks of us as "terrestrial beings" and also as requiring a "cosmic sense" if we are to be fully human and fully Christian. What this text also highlights is the importance of the concept of God to people in the modern world; for many people God as presented in traditional Christianity is irrelevant or meaningless to modern living because God is considered to be an empty symbol, a fragment of a mythical past; this needs to be addressed if Christianity is to have any relevance or speak to the modern world.

Teilhard was not a professional theologian but a scientist and this led to much of his theological output being discounted by Catholic theologians; there was a kind of professional jealousy but also a closing of ranks against Teilhard; although he wrote on theological issues, he often introduced new ideas and ways of expressing them which emanated from his scientific background, training and interests. Many theologians were unused to this new way of doing theology and either misunderstood or misinterpreted Teilhard's views which led to suspicion and even condemnation. The Catholic Church of the time was anything but open-minded and Teilhard, like many other catholic theologians after him, was silenced and sent into exile.

In order to understand Teilhard fully, we have to recognise the character of his writing and become familiar with his use of terminology, often taken from his scientific background; for example, his use of the French word *gènese*, which can be translated as movement, development or evolution in the broad sense. The concept of noogenesis is a good example of the use of quasi-scientific terminology for an idea which has much more than a scientific meaning.

Another important point in understanding Teilhard is the change in the way he writes in different essays and at different times during his career. In the early essays he writes very much in a poetic style and some of his ways of expressing ideas have the mark of a mystic; in later essays he is much more measured in his writing and offers a much more logical form of expression. This is important to remember in reading Teilhard. Another feature of his writing is his mixture of traditional theological terminology and neologisms which betray his scientific career. So, Teilhard may not be an easy read for many but nevertheless rewards those who persevere with his peculiar expressive traits.

It is for this reason that it is difficult to locate Teilhard as a writer and thinker; he is at once a philosopher, a theologian, a spiritual writer, a mystic, a scientist and a social commentator. Basically, he was a deeply religious man who happened to be a scientist and who saw his mission to help others see the world as he did; as a scientist he was aware of the need to present Christianity to a world that often did not recognise God or religion as relevant in the modern world, hence his very characteristic ways of expressing Christian thinking. For his fellow Christians he wanted to show them how they could be fully human and worldly and fully Christian and religious; this was the major thrust of Le Milieu Divin, where he sets out a form of spirituality that embraces material reality and the concerns of the world in a positive and dynamic fashion.

In many ways, Teilhard was a prophet and visionary, introducing a new way of seeing things and of expressing the truths of faith. He opened up new vistas and possibilities but not always in minute detail. Inevitably, he did not complete the picture and it was left to others to fill in the details and to take his ideas forward. Much of this has been done since his death. Unfortunately, because of his relative isolation in China he did not have the opportunity during his life to enter into dialogue with other theologians, which might have allowed him to hone his thinking and lead to a more mature and precise expression of his vision. Despite this, he has left us a tremendous body of writing from which we can develop insights and ways of approach which will enrich our thinking and enhance our understanding of the Christian task. Many of his insights were incorporated in the theology of Vatican II and we will recognise some of these as we discuss his theology and spirituality in the following chapters.

Teilhard's Theological Vision

Teilhard's Christian vision is inspired primarily by the New Testament texts from St Paul, but also from the Prologue to the Gospel of St John, which put Christ at the centre of God's plan for creation and humanity. In particular it is the concept of the Cosmic Christ and the cosmic character of salvation which Teilhard underlines and puts at the very heart of his theology; in this respect it may be more accurate to speak of his Christology for Teilhard's vision is essentially Christ-centred, encompassing the Christ of the Incarnation, the coming of God's presence into the creative process in the person of Jesus Christ, and the Cosmic Risen Christ who brings God's creative plan to fulfilment at the Second Coming, the Parousia.

In *Cosmic Life*, written in 1916, Teilhard is at pains to point out our relationship to the earth with which we share in the creative process initiated by God. While he does not use the term "creation centred theology" as it is used today, in reality his theological vision provides a basis for much that this theology suggests as a starting point for theological thinking. For Teilhard, God is viewed primarily as Creator, the source of all life, a God who freely gives of the divine self in the gift of creation, understood as encompassing the entire universe in all its vastness and complexity and the varying levels of creation culminating in humanity.

The starting point for Teilhard, then, is the creative plan of God centred on Christ which is fulfilled through the evolutionary process, God's own way of effecting the divine will to share the divine life issuing out of the Trinitarian source of love. Because God has chosen to create through an evolutionary process, Teilhard can speak of evolution as holy and our own salvation as bound up with the destiny of the universe. Thus we cannot separate ourselves from the rest of created reality or from the material universe, cocoon ourselves in some form of spiritual isolation. We are "terrestrial beings". It is on these basic premises that Teilhard builds his Christian vision and develops a spirituality that is at the same time a form of Christian humanism.

Towards the end of his time in China he was visited by an Italian Franciscan theologian, Fr Allegra, who introduced him to the theology of Blessed John Duns Scotus. Teilhard was fascinated by what Fr Allegra had to say about Scotus' views on the position of Christ in the economy of salvation. Scotus and the Franciscan theology that he inspired teaches that Christ did not become incarnate as a result of the Fall in order to repair the damage done to God's plan by human sin; for Scotus, Christ was part of the plan of God from the very beginning and the whole of creation had Christ as its purpose and goal; God's creation was FOR Christ. So, for Scotus, Christ would have become incarnate even if human sin had not taken place. Teilhard saw that this dovetailed with his own understanding of the cosmic texts of St Paul; Christ has a truly cosmic significance. So, Teilhard emphasises, with Duns Scotus and the Franciscan tradition, the creative rather than the purely redemptive role of Christ, which has been the major theological thrust of Catholic theology from medi-aeval times right up to the present. One unfortunate consequence of this totally redemptive theology has been an emphasis on sin and our need for redemption and all the consequent negative attitudes to material reality and the world. Teihard pre-empted much of modern theology's return to the themes of creation and its attempts to present a more positive, creation-centred vision of Christian living which is more attuned to a dynamic, forward looking outlook.

Like St Irenaeus before him, Teilhard sees humanity as a work for completion, as created imperfect but destined to perfection rather than as trying to gain a lost perfection as a result of the Fall. Irenaeus speaks of "the Glory of God, humanity fully alive", suggesting that we are to advance from being a partial reflection (image) of God to become the glory of God(likeness). This envisages a gradual development of humanity towards fulfilment; it is a more positive and encouraging vision, acknowledging that we are not yet perfect but have the seed of perfection which Christ will bring to fulfilment. Teilhard's spirituality clearly embraces this view of human destiny; God is not a God that needs to be appeased or offered sacrifice for sin but rather is a God who offers fulfilment within the divine creative plan and calls for human response to this grace-filled offer. Engagement with God's creative venture in a spirit of thanksgiving and total response is the essence of Christian life and calling; it is a positive vision which is much more appealing than one which emphasises sin and repentance and wariness of the world we live in. For sure, we often fail to respond to God due to our human weaknesses and need to ask for forgiveness for our lack of response and commitment but at the same time to ask for renewed strength for the future. Our starting point is not that we are undeserving sinners but that we are God's creation out of love; to present ourselves as poor sinners in some ways diminishes the goodness of God. God is aware of our frailty, for God made us as incomplete creatures, but with the potential to be God's completed work. The New Testament speaks of sin as 'missing the mark', as failing to reach our God given potential, failing to respond to God's call to progress in love. This way of understanding the human venture and the nature of God's gift makes all the difference to the way in which we view our Christian calling and the way in which we engage with God, with others and with the world as a whole. In today's world it is also an important element of ecological awareness and commitment.

It could be argued that there has been a paradigm shift in the way we understand God, our relationship to God and God's creation and this necessitates a new way of living our Christian life and calling. The past century has seen immeasurable change in human communications, technology, social interaction and the emergence of a truly global community. We can no longer live as we did in the past; the gospel has to be preached to a new age, as Teilhard recognised as far back as 1919, and this requires a new vision.

While Teilhard puts the cosmic Christ at the centre of his theology and in this respect always looks forward to the Risen Christ who calls him from the future (the Parousia), the insertion of God's presence in the world in a very potent way (the Incarnation) is seen as an important milestone in the divine creative process. For Teilhard, the cosmic Christ is the same Christ, the man Jesus, who came into this world 2000 years ago. Although the historical Jesus of the Gospels does not figure heavily in Teilhard's writings, in his personal spirituality he had a great devotion to the heart of Christ as symbol of God's love, which he learned from his mother at an early age, and as a Jesuit he would have read the scriptures assiduously and meditated on the life and teaching of the Jesus of the Gospels during his annual Spiritual Exercises. In addition, central to his life as a priest was the celebration of the Eucharist which was a fundamental element of his theology and spirituality. For Teilhard the Eucharist was the foundation of the Church and of Christian life; it was in the Eucharist that the presence of God in Christ was at its highest and gradually permeated creation over the duration of history. As evolution progresses, Christ animates and inspires this process gradually bringing it to fulfilment. This is what Teilhard calls the Christification of matter and the universe and it is effected through the Eucharist and our participation in it, whereby Christ, through us, becomes a part of our world and his power and values permeate creation, gradually bringing it to perfection. The Christ of the Eucharist is the Risen Christ and this links the Eucharist with the Parousia, the end of history, the Pleroma or fullness of God. The Eucharist does not so much look back to the Passion and Death of Jesus in a purely redemptive fashion but rather looks forward to the Risen Christ of Glory beckoning us from the future. While the Passion and Death remind us of the inevitable suffering to be endured during life it is completed in the Resurrection. These cannot be separated; but suffering is not something to be sought but rather represents the effort required to fully engage with the responsibilities of the Christian in the world. If we fully commit ourselves to God's creative work then we will inevitably meet challenge and obstacles which will demand sacrifice – this is the true significance of suffering.

In essence, Teilhard provides a forward-looking vision, which embraces a full acceptance of our place in an evolving world and a positive attitude, buoyed up by the figure of the Risen Jesus who calls to us from the future. It is this figure of the Risen Christ who is at the centre of our Christian life, offering hope and promise. How this vision might be envisaged in more detail we will consider in the next section where we look at Teilhard's spirituality.

CHAPTER SEVEN

Teilhard's Spirituality

Teilhard completed *Le Milieu Divin* (The Divine Milieu) in 1927 while in China as a summary of his vision for Christian living. He was surrounded by fellow scientists, few of whom shared his Christian faith, and in writing this volume he was acutely aware of the need to reach out to those on the periphery of the church and organised religion and to those who needed to be convinced of the importance of faith, the church and most importantly God. It was a form of Christian humanism and an earthly, worldly spirituality that he thus presents for our consideration. While he retained much of what we might call traditional Christian spirituality, he puts it into an evolutionary world view context which highlights its immediacy and developmental character. In the following pages I will outline the elements of *Le Milieu Divin* and link them to the wider Christian vision and spirituality he advocates in his writings as a whole.

Teilhard begins by facing the dilemma felt by many: do I follow the way of prayer and devotion and consider 'the world' as a distraction to following God's way, or do I abandon any attempt to live a life of faith and concentrate on being a fully human person engaged in the demands of life in society? Or, thirdly, do I live a kind of fractured, schizophrenic life in which neither God nor the world demand our full attention. He suggests two possible answers to this dilemma, one a partial and another more complete solution. The partial answer consists in considering human action as having no value other than the intention which directs it. We will all no doubt be familiar with the notion of 'good intentions' and of the practice of 'offering up' all that we will do on a daily basis to God, so that all that we do may be 'for God'. In this way, we hope that all our activity will be of significance for salvation and that we will be faithful to our worldly vocation.

Teilhard rejects this solution for it lacks "the achievement which our spiritual peace and joy so imperiously demand" and he continues:

"The divinization of our effort by the value of the intentions put into it infuses a priceless soul into all our actions; but it does not confer the hope of resurrection upon their bodies . . . It is certainly a very great thing to think that, if we love God, something of our inner activity...will never be lost. But will not the very work of our minds, our hearts and our hands – our achievements, our work . . . – will not this, too, in some way be 'eternalized' and saved?" (MD 56)

Teilhard puts forward a final solution which imparts a positive value on all our human activity and which is the basis of his understanding of Christian life as he himself lived it and is fully explained in the rest of the book. This approach to the problem is rooted in Teilhard's concept of God and God's relationship to the world. In much of traditional theology God is seen as 'outside' the created world, as it were looking down on creation, directing it or sustaining it from this vantage point. Teilhard sees God as **within** the creative process, not exterior to it, and thus everything is suffused by God's creative influence. The incarnation underlies this interiority of God:

"In fact, through the unceasing operation of the Incarnation, the divine so thoroughly penetrates all our creaturely energies that, to meet it and lay hold on it, we could not find a more fitting setting than that of our action." (MD 62)

Perhaps we too often think of the incarnation merely as the coming of God in the person of the Jesus of history rather than as the coming of God into the very depths of material reality and the creative venture. Because he sees God's relationship to creation in this way Teilhard considers **every created action** as having intrinsic meaning and value and as of salvific significance. God did not create the world and its materiality purely as a means or pretext for spiritual activity but rather as a significant vehicle of divine creativity and therefore we have to value creation in its entirety as the God given means of divine self-giving. Throughout his writings Teilhard is at pains to draw out the implications of this in his 'spirituality of human effort' which is specifically dealt with in *Le Milieu Divin*. What he tried to do was to link all aspects of human activity to the spiritual quest, in such a way that there was no rupture between 'spiritual life/christian life' and human

life tout court. In many ways this is the beauty of his teaching and
what has captured the imagination of so many theologians, thinkers
and ordinary Christians seeking a meaningful existence as both
humans and people of faith in a world that offers both positive
challenge and negative diversion for a fulfilling existence.

Central to Teilhard's thinking is the concept of the Divine Milieu,
which became the title of his signature writing. If we see God as
within and interior to reality, rather than as exterior and 'other
worldly' in a remote fashion, it is clear that the whole universe is
undergirded by God's influence, God is the inner force or energy of
everything. Whether we are conscious of it or not we are subject in
some way to the divine influence in all that we do and what happens
to us. We are encircled by the power and love of God in such a way
that we continually live in God's presence and Teilhard calls this all-
encompassing presence the divine milieu. We live in the divine milieu
and our life is a call to become conscious of this presence in all that
we do and to make God's presence a visible reality in our lives. This
not only makes God a reality for us but for others, for all those with
whom we come in contact. This is the basis of our mission as
Christians, to bring Christ to the world.

The notion of living in the divine milieu is truly captivating and
brings God closer to us but is also the key to understanding how all
our actions have saving significance and therefore of value in themselves. This is at the very heart of Teilhard's thinking and is his most
original contribution to Christian spirituality. In *Le Milieu Divin* he
explains his thinking on these matters in very concrete terms:

"It is through the collaboration which he stimulates in us that
Christ, starting from all created things, is consummated and attains his
plenitude . . . With each one of our works, we labour, separately, but
no less really, to build the Pleroma; that is, we bring to Christ a little
completion. Every one of our works, by its more or less remote or
direct effect on the spiritual world, helps to perfect Christ in his
mystical totality" (MD 62). He underlines this further when he says:

"God, in all that is most living and incarnate in him, is not
distanced from us, altogether apart from the world we see,
touch, hear, smell and taste around us. Rather he awaits us every
instant in our action, in the work of the moment. There is a
sense in which he is at the top of my pen, my spade, my brush,

my needle – of my heart and of my mind. By pressing the stroke, the line, or the stitch, on which I am engaged, to its ultimate natural finish, I shall lay hold of this last end towards which my most interior will tends." (MD 64).

What Teilhard is saying here is that we need to do everything to the best of our ability, fulfil each of our obligations without stint, and in such a way that we are truly 'building God's world', a world in which the values of truth and holiness are realized. In many ways Teilhard follows the teaching of St Therese of Lisieux who did all the small things, all the things required of her, to their fullest possible extent. Teilhardian spirituality is about being authentic human beings, fulfilling our duties in all areas of our life with complete dedication and purity of heart. This will require selflessness and awareness of others; it is what Teilhard calls an 'ascesis of effort', a readiness to serve the needs of the world around us whatever the cost. What is appealing about this way of viewing things is that it makes the demands of everyday living in whatever situation we find ourselves the major focus of our spiritual life and development; we do not need to look for 'extras' in order to fulfil our spiritual calling. If we do everything our life situation in all its various elements asks of us then we will meet challenges, self-sacrifice and even suffering. This is the price of building God's world and the cross of Jesus is the supreme example of such an effort.

Later in *Le Milieu Divin* Teilhard speaks about some of the practical aspects of Christian life and shows how all elements of our life, our personal make up and the situations we encounter, have a place in our spiritual development. He speaks of our activities and passivities and how they are part of how we respond to God and to God's call to mission in the world. Our activities are those things we do, our passivities are the things that happen to us. We may consider what we do, our activities, as being more important than what happens to us but both are equally important in our efforts to respond to God in daily life. He recognises that each of us has been made very differently, we have varying natural talents and personal dispositions, strengths and weaknesses, and encounter different life situations and challenges, but all are part of God's providence, they reflect different ways in which God gifts life to us. We have to become aware of ourselves, understand our own personal circumstances of life, for it is in these that we are given the opportunities and the environment within which we share the God-given task of making the divine presence a reality in our world. Self awareness and daily reflection on our activity and relationships is required if we are to respond fully to God's call.. and we have to use both our strengths and our weaknesses in the service of God as these have been given to us as part of our human make-up. Providence has ensured that whatever our station in life and the range of our gifts we are able to contribute in a positive fashion to the work of 'building God's world'. There may be a temptation to neglect or discount situations in our life which appear to be negative or as impediments to doing positive work for God, for the church, even for society as a whole; what Teilhard suggests is that even those aspects of life that may appear mundane or of little outward significance can still be a means of making God's presence felt. The life of the spirit is to be found in the earthly, material realities of life and not in trying to lift above them to reach a more spiritual realm. The model here is Jesus himself, who showed the love of the Father for humanity in every aspect of his life: his life, teaching, suffering and death. This is a thoroughly incarnational approach to Christian living. We have to bring God's presence into every created reality and this may mean doing great things or doing the very small and insignificant for they are all part of the patchwork of creation that God has gifted us.

Thus, we have to bring God's creative presence to the whole of our life as we experience it; in real terms this means fulfilling our obligations as family member, worker, neighbour and global citizen using all the talents given to us by God, even what we see as weaknesses.

The teaching of *Le Milieu Divin* is in many ways quite traditional in emphasizing the importance of doing the little things to the full, but it is the context within which this is set which is new and inspiring. We are all seen as co-creators of God's world in such a way that literally **everything** has a saving significance, contributing to the ongoing work of divine creativity. God did not put us in this world merely to work out our salvation irrespective of the destiny of the world of creation; rather he created a world within which we are given the tremendous dignity but also consequent responsibility of bringing this work to its fulfilment, leading to the final crowning of this tremendous venture at the victory of the Risen Christ at the end of time. It is this sublime context that gives our humble lives such depth of meaning and significance and we have to grasp it fully in faith and trust in the knowledge that God will bring all things including ourselves to their ultimate perfection. What a task and what a prospect !!

CHAPTER EIGHT

Toward the Future
A Summary

In this book I have tried to outline an approach to Christian living and spirituality in a modern, evolutionary world with reference to the work of Teilhard de Chardin and here I would like bring all the various elements together by way of a summary and practical conclusion.

The documents of Vatican II and the theology underlying it provided a vision which was characterised as biblically based, forward-looking, dynamic, integrated and oriented to effective mission to the world. There was also an emphasis on the participation of every person, of whatever status, in the worship, liturgy and activity of the Church towards the fulfilment of their baptismal priesthood in the world of their experience.

While great steps have been taken to make this vision a reality, there is still much to be done as recent moves to return to the practices of the past and to dogmatic correctness has shown; the efforts of Pope Francis to present a more open Church and environmental awareness have likewise faced much opposition from a small but powerful minority. Despite these set-backs we need to persevere in our efforts to offer a viable programme of evangelisation and to show its effectiveness and attraction by living it out in our daily lives.

So how can we do this? There are several areas of faith and practice which are fundamental and I would like to suggest some points for reflection. They are not presented in any particular order of importance and are taken from biblical sources and from the reflections of Teilhard de Chardin, Thomas Berry and other modern interpreters.

Firstly, we need to keep in the forefront of our mind the awareness of the earth as our mother and as the source of our life and livelihood. This requires us to respect the needs of the earth, our natural environment as well as other creatures on earth; they form part of a delicate system of life which supports us all. We must use the earth's resources in such a way that they are sustainable and available to all around the world. We should consider our use of food and other material goods in a spirit of humility and poverty, ready to share what we have with others in need and reflect on the extent of our personal possessions. This is a very personal area of decision and can only be reached after prayerful and collaborative reflection; our response will depend on the depth of our commitment to the Lord's call. In practical terms, we need to live in an environmentally sensitive way, engaging in a responsible life-style and cooperating in any collective efforts to preserve ecological balance and sustainability. All these elements will express our recognition of the reciprocity of the earth–human relationship and of the God-givenness of the created order. In this context, we are divinely mandated to care for the earth, our common mother in the words of Pope Francis.

A second area for reflection is the way in which ecological aware-ness and life-style are an important part of our way of responding to the Gospel message as presented by Jesus. If we consider what Jesus says about the kingdom, the very heart of his message, we see how it makes demands on us in our world of today. The kingdom of God is not so much a place or state so much as a set of values which sum up Jesus' teaching: it turns the normally accepted values upside down – the first will be last and the last will be first. The kingdom is about growth from small beginnings; the arrival of a new age; the mercy of God; the moment of crisis, the Kairos moment, when we must decide whether to accept the challenge of Jesus to change our way of life – metanoia, which can mean repentance or more accurately a complete change of life, an about-turn in our attitudes. While it is a personal challenge it has implications for not only the individual but for social and political structures, for all those with whom we come into contact. Jesus' teaching about the kingdom is presented mostly in parables and these are simple but profound stories taken from everyday life where the normal rules and conditions are overturned and the listeners are confronted with a decision – to accept the topsy-turvy logic and put complete faith in God. Jesus puts these stories before us all and basically says: "if the cap fits, wear it". We need to engage with the parables on a regular basis and ponder on the demands of the kingdom whose values are essential to our Christian life. Of course, reflection on the scriptures should be a daily practice, in which we carefully listen to the Spirit speaking to us through the revealed Word.

Teilhard speaks frequently about seeing and listening as two essential characteristics of Christian life. He saw things in the world around him and recognised their inner meaning and such were their power and influence on him that he wanted to share them with others; his writings were an attempt to share his vision of reality with others as he believed they could enrich their own understanding. But Teilhard did not just see things he also listened to them; his awareness of the presence of God in the whole of reality taught him to listen carefully to all that he saw around him in order to understand their significance and draw any lesson or receive any challenge they offered. This notion of seeing and listening as a two-fold engagement with reality is an important aspect of our awareness of the Spirit leading us; the Spirit often speaks in the hidden depths, in the silence of reality and rarely in a loud, bold fashion. So, the practice of reflective, expectant seeing and listening should form part of our 'reading the signs of the times' in our world, leading to the transformation of the world, the building of God's world. This is an ability that has to be carefully and persistently nurtured and developed in order for us to be effective in our mission as Christians.

All the above elements need to become part of our daily practice and inspire all our prayer, worship and activity. We all live very different lives and we need to gradually carve out our own personal patterns of living, when we pray, when we engage with the scriptures, how we weave all these various activities and responsibilities into a meaningful and manageable routine. Each and every item in our daily routine has its own importance in the grand scheme of things and what matters ultimately is that all are seen as ways of living in the presence of God. Teilhard had a very real awareness of God in all that he did but at the same time he put his complete effort into whatever he was doing; whether he was saying mass, researching, exploring the desert, teaching students or conversing with friends or colleagues. Those who knew him attested to the fact that he always appeared to be totally immersed in what tasks he had and that even when he spoke to people he gave them his complete attention, no matter who they were. He was no 'holy Joe', concerned only with 'holy things', with his head always in a prayer book. He had his times of prayer and worship which were important to him as the sources of his awareness of God but he saw his life as fully integrated in which each element was of equal value.

An interesting fact relating to Teilhard's daily routine is that, while most Jesuit priests practised the examen, or reflection on their day, at night time, when the day was over, Teilhard did his first thing in the morning. He would think about all that he was going to do in some detail and incorporate it all into the offering of his day to God, so that all was done with the right intention. This was not just a short prayer offering the day to God in a general way but a considered reflection on the nature of his work, the people he would meet and work with; this underlines the seriousness Teilhard attached to daily activity of all kinds as his involvement in and dedication to what he calls 'building God's world'. This approach to our daily examination of conscience and reflection on our relationship to God is a way of ensuring that we maintain an awareness of the nature of our Christian life and calling. It is also an important step on the way to 'living in the divine milieu', being conscious of the fact that God is present at the heart of everything and in this way we can meet God in all that we do. Gradually we become acutely aware of our relationship to God at all times. We have a very striking example of this in the life of Jesus who was always in touch with his Father in prayer and this relationship was at the heart of all that he said and did – he is always talking about doing his Father's will and only speaking the message he receives from the Father.

Teilhard was certainly a man of prayer, some would say a mystic, and the fruit of his prayer infiltrated every corner of his existence. He speaks of living in the divine milieu, the real but mysterious presence of God at the heart of reality, and this constantly reminds him of his call to collaborate with God in the great work of divine creativity, the evolutionary process within which Christ is gradually becoming ever-more present until he will be fully revealed as the meaning and purpose of creation – the Cosmic Christ – at the end of history, the Parousia. Because of the inextricable link between human activity and the creative work of God Teilhard saw literally all human endeavour as holy. Being a good parent, a conscientious artisan, a talented artist, a valued neighbour – in all the roles we play in daily life we contribute to the creative work of God and build God's world towards its completion in Christ. Therefore, we have to do everything with the same purpose, intensity and dedication, nothing is without a significance in the greater plan of God. Teilhard said that what we must do is to complete everything, even the most seemingly insignificant act, to its completion and to the best of our ability; this was our salvation. Prayer and worship are essential as the source and inspiration of our devotion to the work of God but they do not take the place of our contribution to building God's world in all the things we do within our daily life and responsibilities. This is the bottom line.

While we may not have the spiritual insight or deep awareness of God to the same degree that Teilhard had, he was after all an exceptional and unique individual, but we can still aspire to his ideal in our own way. Basically, his form of spirituality is very simple, very much like St Therese of Lisieux, which consists in doing everything to the best of our ability, not cutting corners or dismissing the things we least like doing but going the extra mile. This requires complete dedication and being prepared to accept the sacrifices which may be needed in fulfilling our responsibilities in life. What makes Teilhard's spiritual way different is the context within which he sets it, namely the completion of the cosmic plan of God in which we have an inalienable responsibility as co-creators in bringing God's plan to fulfilment in Christ.

Two virtues which Teilhard lived and deemed as essential to this work were fidelity and purity. Fidelity was the firm resolve to remain faithful to his task as a personal response to God's call and to trust in the help and grace of God to achieve this. In all his brushes with Church authority and the suffering and mental strain this involved, he remained faithful to his religious superiors, to the Church leaders and to his priestly calling and scientific research. When he speaks of purity, or purity of intention, he does not restrict this to matters of sexuality or chastity but rather means purity of intention in all we do and in all aspects of our life. It is about personal honesty, being genuine in our motives, dedicating ourselves completely to what is set before us and doing things for the right motives in a spirit of humility and selflessness. It is also about seeing everything in relation to God and our relationship to God, God's presence in all things.

Such is the character of Christian spirituality in an evolving world and the vision provided by Teilhard. Hopefully these reflections will be helpful for all those who aspire to a meaningful and fulfilling Christian life in a world that is both a challenge and an enthralling prospect.

Appendix
Reading Teilhard on
'The Christian in the World'

In reading these texts we have to remember, firstly, that they were written at different times, from 1916 to 1955, during different phases of his life, and thus will represent slightly different emphases in his thinking. Secondly, they were published as they had been left by Teilhard, without any editing prior to publication as they were only begun to be published after his death. Many of his writings were first thoughts on the topic and not polished essays – had he been given the opportunity to discuss his ideas openly with others, especially theologians, they may well have been presented in a more mature fashion. For all that, his words are full of personal conviction and enthusiasm, even emotional engagement; he has his own characteristic style and modes of expression which derive from his mystical insight in his earlier essays and his scientific background in the later ones, which can be both challenging and thought provoking. Finally, written prior to our modern concern for gender equality, his use of 'man/men' should be read as also referring to women. The texts used are those of the original English translations which do not attempt to address these issues. Teilhard was very much aware of the place of women in society and social discourse and was very unusual as a priest in his days in the number of women with whom he communicated and discussed religious and other issues, including his cousin Marguerite Teilhard-Chambon, the artist Lucille Swan, Ida Treat an American social and philosophical thinker, Rhoda de Terra the wife of one of his fellow palaeontologists, Leontine Zanta a Parisian philosopher and finally Jeanne Mortier to whom he entrusted all his writings for publication after his death. Teilhard often said that his contact with women had had a beneficial and fruitful influence on his thinking.

The Christian in the World

Here I provide a summary of Teilhard's thinking in his own words. While the selection and presentation of his words are mine I feel they substantially represent Teilhard's own vision. In order to understand something of the development and progression of his thinking I offer a brief comment on each section, pointing up some of the emphases and contextual issues.

For references to *The Divine Milieu* (DM) and *The Human Phenomenon* (PM), the first reference is to the original edition and in brackets to the new translation from Sussex Academic Press.

Teilhard begins by reading the texts of St Paul and other New Testament texts, which he read as a man with a scientific mind. It was these biblical insights that fired his imagination and led to the development of his Christian vision and is an important point to keep in mind – he begins with the scriptures.

A. New Testament Texts
Romans 8, 19; 8, 22–23
Ephesians 1, 9–10; 1, 23; 3, 9–11; 3, 16–19; 4, 10–13
Philippians 2, 9–11; 3, 20
Colossians 1, 15–20; 2, 9; 3, 11

In relation to the texts from the New Testament, Teilhard reminds us that each generation reads the scriptures in different ways, with different eyes and different questions. It is thus that nowadays these so-called cosmic texts are understood differently by the people of New Testament times, those in the Middle Ages and subsequent centuries. The cosmic significance of Christ for modern readers takes on a new meaning and leads to a magnificent and inspiring vision. This reminds us of both the historical boundedness and timelessness of the scriptures and our need to dialogue with the scriptural witness in order to retain and develop an authentic Christian faith.

WTW/CL 58   TF / AW 98   HM/C 93

B. The World Today
Teilhard speaks about the world of today, our contemporary world, and draws attention to the fact that we live in a world that has changed and continues to do so. Science and technology have drastically

changed the way in which we view and understand the world we live in; what is of particular importance is that the world is now seen as dynamic, evolving, a movement or process rather than the static universe of the past. The world is revealed to us as immense and as dynamic, in a process of becoming. We thus need to rethink the categories of faith and our concept of God in the light of our changed world view. One aspect of this new perception is the way in which we are related to the world, our cosmic awareness. Teilhard sees us as essentially cosmic in our make-up and that we can only be fully Christian if we are fully human and cosmic. Being a Christian does not mean leaving the world but engaging with it, seeking God in and through the world.

TF/SM 14–15   FM/GO 58–59   FM/HP 261–2
WTW/SW 188–9   WTW/FC 250–1
HM/NPG 220   HM/MAC 117–18

One feature of the world is its evolutionary character, which is recognised in what Teilhard refers to as the law of complexity-consciousness, whereby as things become more complex they are endowed with a greater degree of awareness. In their self-consciousness humans are the highest form of life and thus represent the most important element in the world process, giving humanity a special place and role in the evolutionary plan of God. Humans are the self-consciousness of the universe and this makes them the leading shoot in the evolutionary tree, placing a great responsibility on them for the future of the planet. Since Teilhard's death this aspect of his thinking has been used as a basis for ecological theology.

MD 58–59 (16–17)   WTW/CL 14–15
AE/RSP 272   HM/MIP 143
WTW/MM 130

Of course, since Teilhard's death our understanding of the world has been tremendously enhanced through the insights of astronomy and cosmology and the development of human society has been much influenced by the modern means of communication particularly such things as the internet and the world wide web; if Teilhard were alive today he would have fully embraced these new movements as part of his understanding of the world. In his concept of noogenesis, the development of mind, the instantaneous and world-wide communication that we experience today would have found a profound expression.

Teilhard's concept of creative union underlines the general notion of a convergence towards unity; the relationship of matter and spirit that it presupposes may be helpful in leading to an acceptance of the world as central to Christian life and practice. Teilhard suggests that evolution is leading to an end point which he calls Omega Point which will be the coming together of all things in God, the fulfilment of God's plan. This will coincide with the initiative of God in the Second Coming of Christ, the Parousia. If evolution is moving towards a point of convergence, this point must be a transcendent principle that is able to effect the completion of the process and also possess the power and magnetism to effect the movement towards fulfilment. Omega is thus seen to be a divine principle; ultimately it is the Risen Christ, the transforming power of God in the world. But this is also rooted in the Incarnation, the coming into the world of the divine principle, Jesus Christ. Teilhard stresses the importance of linking the Cosmic Christ with the person of Jesus who entered our history; the Cosmic Christ is in continuity with the incarnate Christ, Jesus the man. In the same way, Teilhard in many of his essays under-lines the importance of matter in relation to spirit; they are not in opposition but indissolubly linked with each other. As the earthly Jesus leads us to the Risen, Cosmic Christ, so earthly matter is the ground of spirit. Teilhard uses the example of the relationship of inhalation and exhalation in the breathing process to show how matter and spirit relate to each other in the process of our divinisation.

SC/MU 45   SC/MU 51   HM/NM 227
SC/MU 50   MPN 15–16

If God created the world, Teilhard argues, then it must have value in itself and not be a mere chance element or a whim. This being the case, the material world cannot be discounted in our progress toward God and in emphasising the importance of being immersed in the world rather than seeing it as a temptation or diversion from our spiritual progress, Teilhard departs from many previous forms of spirituality and offers us a new vision which is much more attuned to life in the world today. Having placed Christian existence within an evolutionary, cosmic context Teilhard leads us on to a reflection on the nature of Christian living within this dynamic, changing world.

C. God and the World

Teilhard underlines the real significance of the world and matter for Christian living, for creation is an ongoing process, God's continuing creativity is present in and among us.

CE/HIB 132   MD 139(102)   MD 114(75)
MD 64(22–3) WTW/CL 61   WTW/MM 133

Furthermore, because creation is continuing, God's presence can never be fully revealed; it is a source of constant novelty and we can really speak of a "God of surprises". God's active presence is hidden and yet revealed in the experiences and activities of our lives, which Teilhard describes as our activities (the things we do) and our passivities (the things that happen to us and over which we may not have full control). Whether active or passive, our life experience is the way in which God and the divine influence enters our life and so the whole of our life, everything we do or are subject to, is the means whereby God reaches us and we reach God. Teilhard speaks of the Divine Milieu (which is also the title of his essay on spirituality) by which he means the presence of God and God's influence in the creative enterprise which is our world and in the totality of human experience. In this respect, literally nothing is without spiritual significance and we constantly live in the divine milieu. Reflection on this point will open our minds to the importance of doing everything in and for God as part of participation in God's continuing creativity.

Central to our understanding of the creative process is an acceptance of the role of the Cosmic, Risen Christ in its progress through history. Teilhard points out that from the very beginning Christ is the centre and purpose of God's plan. In the liturgy Christ is called 'Christ the King'; Teilhard would prefer to speak of the Cosmic or Universal Christ as a more accurate title; for many today, kingship is not particularly meaningful, a dated and even negative title and does not do full justice to the role of Christ in the drama of creation.

SC/RCW 189   SC/CS 189
SC/SHSC 166–7   SC/MU 54

Considering ways of understanding the creative process, we can also speak of the "Christification" of the world, the gradual formation of the cosmic Body of Christ, the increasing influence of Christ in the world. Through our relationship and fidelity to Christ and particularly through receiving Christ in the eucharist, we in effect allow Christ to enter the world and influence its progress. In this respect we are true "ambassadors of Christ" as St Paul calls us, as we actively engage in the work of making Christ's presence felt in the world we live in. This fact also shows the importance of us as the active presence of the Church as a vehicle of bringing the influence of Christ to bear on the various elements of human society in its progress through history.

Looking at our lives within this perspective we can see how God's plan can be seen as a process of fulfilment whereby the fullness of God becomes present in creation; this is what St Paul refers to as the "pleroma" or fulness of God, the formation of the Cosmic Body of Christ. It is only as part of this process that we will be saved and in this respect salvation is essentially cosmic and social in character.

SC/NUC 14   CE/FRG 39   SC/SC 34   SC/RCW 125
CE/CE 89   WTW/CL 58–59   CE/PC 70   MD 117(79)
CE/CEV 145–6   CE/HROS 52   SC/MU 63–64   CE/HIB 129
MD 143(106)   MD 62(20)   MD 122(84)   CE/PC 67

It is clear, then, that Teilhard views Christian life within an evolutionary, cosmic and dynamic context. The features of this life are outlined in the following sections.

D. Christian Life and Witness in the World

Firstly, the Christian has to recognise the value of the world and worldly activity so that the entirety of a person's life becomes a holy endeavour and a truly priestly function. However, while acknowledging the reality of the world there is also a need to recognise its incompleteness, the 'not yet' as well as the 'already'. Primacy is thus given to God's action and all human activity has to be subordinated to the Spirit of God and its gift of life. Teilhard often spoke of 'building God's world' to underline the ultimate salvific significance of all human activity; he points out that our lives are not a random happening but the result of providence and divine choice – we are all elements of a grand divine plan of which we only glimpse the shadows but which truly ennobles our participation in the plan.

HE/MS 179   HM/NPG 222   MD 69(27)   MD 97(57)
FM/HP 260   MD 60–61(18)   MD 154(117–18)   HE/SPV 48
SC/MU 67   MD 50(8)   MD 55(12–13) MD 30–1 (91–2)
MD 115(76–7)

While the Christian professes God's presence in the world he/she must constantly seek to sharpen one's sensitivity and awareness of this presence. This is an act of inward seeing which is the result of grace and openness to God's call which is heightened in our prayer life. This meeting with God, the recognition of God's presence in and through the gifts of creation, is the domain of the divine milieu and every Christian is called to live in the divine milieu in the knowledge and consciousness of God's presence to us in every fibre of our being and in every event and circumstance of our life.

Teilhard points to the centrality of the Eucharist in Christian life. The Church gives expression to the essentially social character of Christian faith and to the reality of the Mystical Body of Christ, while the Eucharist realises in a physical, tangible fashion the fact of the Incarnation – Christ's presence in the world of material creation. The Eucharist is thus a heightened moment in the Christification of the world of matter and stands at the centre of Christian living and practice. It is the starting point and source of all missionary activity, of the mission of the church to the world.

HM/MAC 116–17 CE/ICL 165–6
SC/MU 65   MD 126(87–8)

E. Characteristic Features of Christian Life

This is not exhaustive but rather a selection of the most important values and virtues which must be cultivated by anyone who wishes to partake in and contribute to the continuing creativity of God in today's world.

The first priority is that of commitment and choice, a decision to enter into a personal relationship with Jesus Christ. Only thus will we be able to recognise and accept all things as manifestations of God's will for us.

CE/PC 73   LZ 60   MM 66–67

In the Teilhardian perspective the central energy of evolution as a process is love, ultimately the love of God. So, love must be the primary Christian characteristic and it must not remain at the level of pity or succour but must go further and include a passionate dedication to further human progress. In other words, charity must be characterised by a greater REALISM and an awareness of the very structures of human existence. In some ways it is more about being than doing; it is also about seeing love as the primary inspiration of all human activity, both personal and social.

PM 290–1   FM/LP 120   TF/SM 33

Considering the virtues of Christian living, Teilhard views morality from a dynamic perspective and in a social context, going beyond many traditional presentations which view morality and Christian activity from a purely personal viewpoint. For Teilhard morality is concerned with the growth of our capacity to love others and to love the world in a detached and selfless fashion and to attempt all things for the sake of the building of the Kingdom. Morality thus has a distinctly social character and is concerned with our response to others and to the needs of the world about us with all its challenges and aspirations. We cannot afford to be enclosed Christians but rather be open to all that is happening in our world, at a local and global level, willing to go the extra mile for those in need and for the betterment of humanity.

HM/NPG 220   TF/RH 120

Teilhard puts faith and fidelity at the heart of his discussion of Christian living and for him faith is about personal conviction more than about an acceptance of the truths of Christianity. Faith is about openness to what God asks of us and what is required of us in our responsibilities to others and to the world we live in. The activation of this faith he calls fidelity, the determination to make our faith commitment a reality in every circumstance of our life.

MD 134(97)   MD 137–8(100–1)

Along with faith and fidelity, purity of heart is a complete dedication to the things of God; for many, purity of heart might be primarily linked with chastity and the control of sexuality. While Teilhard does not discount the importance of this aspect, for him purity of heart is a much deeper awareness and appreciation of the call of God in our lives, seeing God in all things and a singularity of purpose in following God's call in all the events of our lives without exception. For a person who is pure of heart God becomes everything, the very centre of their life and being.

MD 133–4(95–6)   WTW/SM 107–8

Not unrelated to this form of dedication in faith, fidelity and purity of heart is a need to understand detachment and resignation as practical requirements in the challenges of daily life. They are not negative elements but rather positive aspects of our growth towards God. It is inevitable, says Teilhard, that if we fully embrace the world for God, an acceptance of all things is required – success and failure, personal diminution and disappointment. Attachment and detachment are not alternatives for the Christian but are inseparable companions in our progress in the world and towards God, they are moments in the dialectic that characterises Christian existence, like breathing in and out. In this context, resignation is not a capitulation to the forces of evil or the blind acceptance of everything in a spirit of weak conformity or humble submission but rather the acceptance of God's will once we have done everything in our power to fulfil the task before us. It is at this point that we may well have to undergo suffering and our model here is Jesus and his acceptance of suffering even unto death. However, suffering should not be considered in purely negative terms or merely as satisfaction for sin as is so often the case in Christian thinking. Rather, it should be seen as part of the sometimes painful effort to overcome the forces that militate against the progress of God's work in the world.

TF/SM 32   MD 96(56)

Suffering is the inevitable consequence of the evolutionary process of transformation that is being effected in the world. This also applies to the suffering of Jesus which is not only expiation for sin but also the burden he had to carry on his road to victory. Suffering is not to be accepted as the inevitable will of God but should be overcome if at all possible and only accepted when all efforts to challenge it have been exhausted; at this point we trust in God that ultimate victory can be achieved. Here again, the Christian's attitude must be positive, ready to make every effort to fight evil and suffering trusting fully in God's transforming power.

HE/SPV 50–51   WTW/CL 71   TF/MFV 197–8

The ultimate challenge for us is death and Teilhard sees this as the ultimate "hollowing out" of the individual in order to effect the final transformation by God and we are given hope and assurance of God's transforming power in the resurrection of Jesus, the pledge of our final victory. Death is not to be feared, therefore, but accepted as the final transition to a new life in Christ, the transformation of our bodily life to a glorious body in a risen state. In this respect, our life should be characterised by hope and expectation, looking forward to the Parousia, the Second Coming of Christ and the fulfilment of the whole cosmic drama. The entire Christian life should be parousial in nature, a constant looking forward to the Risen Lord who calls us from ahead and who ensures our final victory.

MD 82(43)   MD 88–9(49–50)

TF/TP 153   MD 151(114)

F. Prayers – A Selection taken from Teilhard's Writings

Teilhard was a man of deep and constant prayer; some would say he was a mystic. His prayerful attitude is caught in many of his writings which are interspersed with some beautiful and inspirational prayers. The references here are to a selection of Teilhard's prayers which may offer inspiration to those who are trying to develop their relationship to God in the depths of their heart. These prayers relate to various aspects of our Christian life as indicated.

For the Divine Milieu	MD 132(94)
For Openness to Christ's influence	WTW/P 216–17
To Christ, Lord of the Cosmos	WTW/CL 69–70
To Love Others	MD 145(108–9)
On Matter	MD 106–7(66–7)
On Christ as Centre of Creation	HU/MW 24–25
In Suffering and Death	WTW/MM 131–2
Of Thanks for God in our Lives	HU/MW 25

Glossary

Complexity-Consciousness
For Teilhard this is the law according to which the inner being of things has a form of awareness in the inanimate and lower orders of creation and develops into sensation and then consciousness and psychological/spiritual power, with more organised and complex organisation as we go up the levels of being, reaching its highest form in humans who have self-consciousness. This is a process of matter becoming more spiritual in the evolutionary process, showing the close interrelationship of matter and spirit. Teilhard speaks of all beings having an inner and outer element, corresponding to material and spiritual.

Creative Union
creation is seen as a process in which initial disorganisation (multiplicity) gradually becomes more organised, leading to the ultimate union of all things. This means that evolution has a direction, is moving toward some kind of completion.

Gènese **(French) the process of development, emergence, movement**
As evolution implies movement it also can be seen as a series of steps toward greater complexity. Each step represents the passing of a threshold. Within this process Teilhard speaks of the first step, the creation of the universe, as cosmogenesis – the development of the cosmos/world. This is followed by the appearance of life in its various forms, from very simple single cells etc to more advanced forms such as plants, insects and animals – this is biogenesis. Animal life reaches a new threshold with the appearance of humans which we call anthropogenesis. As humans develop with their increased brain power and self-consciousness they gradually encircle the earth with a layer of thinking and intelligence which can have an influence on the progress of evolution – this is noogenesis. Teilhard believed that this human

layer of influence would lead to a kind of world consciousness, a coming together of minds which could be a driving force of evolutionary progress. No doubt, if Teilhard were alive today he would see the world wide web as a similar kind of organism. Finally, he saw the ultimate step in the evolutionary process as the completion of the creative enterprise by Christ, at the end of time. This is Christogenesis, Christ fulfilling the universe as the Cosmic Christ.

Immanence – Transcendence

These are the two poles of God's relationship to the world as understood by traditional theology and philosophy. On the one hand God is completely other, totally above us and creation, all powerful and unreachable – he is transcendent. However, God also sustains everything as creator and in this respect is within all things in some mysterious way. This is God's immanence. Throughout Christian history there has always been an attempt to balance these two aspects, at times one has been emphasised rather than the other. In an evolutionary world view context as envisaged by Teilhard immanence is perhaps given greater emphasis.

Modernism

This was a movement, particularly in France, during the late 19th century which challenged the static, essentialist and hierarchical aspects of Catholic thinking and was condemned by the Church as holding heretical views. For many in the Church, some of Teilhard's views were too close to modernist thinking and hence the draconian measures taken against him.

The Divine Milieu

By this Teilhard meant the presence of God in the world as the source and inspiration of all creation and the creative process. He speaks about 'living in the divine milieu' at all times, in other words being aware of God's presence in all we do and meet in life. This emphasises the immanence of God.

Metanoia

This term is found in the Gospels and is often translated as 'repentence'. Jesus calls for metanoia in his followers; what he was asking for was a change of heart, a complete reversal of our attitudes and thinking in order to follow him and his radical programme; Metanoia is this change, rather than repentance as such, though it may also require this.

Omega

In order for evolution to reach its completion Teilhard believed that there had to be a force or element at its centre which acts as its motive force and the guarantee of its success. This force is Omega, which acts as an attractive force within evolution and towards which it moves – the Omega Point. For Teilhard Omega can be identified with the Cosmic Christ. Thus, Christ is Omega, the energy, motive force and purpose or end of evolution.

Theandric

Theos is the Greek for God/divine, so this word is used to refer to Christ's activity as both human and divine. During his life Christ acted as a human person but at the same time he was God. This is an issue that has spawned many theological controversies and speculation. It is important to understand that Teilhard sees an identification of the Christ of the Gospels, the human Jesus, and the Cosmic Christ. There is a direct link between the Incarnation of the Word (the coming of the divine Christ as a human), the Life and Teaching, the Death and Resurrection of Jesus, the Sending of the Spirit at Pentecost and the coming of Christ at the end of time.

The Passibility of God

This means the ability of God to suffer as a result of human sin and failure to follow Gods' ways. In traditional theology God is considered as impassable and unable to be affected by human actions. However, process philosophy which was first introduced by Alfred North Whitehead in the early part of the 20th century and taken up by a number of theologians in America in the 1960s, believes that God, in opening the divine to creation, thereby opened it to possible rejection by humans who had been created with free will. Teilhard follows this thinking to some extent though he had already suggested this line of thinking before process theology became popular. This form of thinking is also referred to as pan-entheism, God in all things, as opposed to pantheism which sees God and all things as the same entity, with no distinction.

Parousia/Pleroma

The Parousia is the revelation of Christ at the end of time, often referred to as the Second Coming of Christ, which figures in St Paul's Epistles to the Colossians and Ephesians – his cosmic theology. This event will bring creation to its fulfilment and thus glorify God; in some ways this will add to the glory of God and represent God's fulness/pleroma.

Paradigm

A paradigm is a way of looking at things, an essential mind-set, such as believing the earth is flat or that the sun goes round the earth. A paradigm change was required when astronomy proved that the earth moves around the sun – and it caused mayhem in the church because it seemed to conflict with the biblical viewpoint. Teilhard suggests that a paradigm shift is required in order to appreciate fully the implications of evolutionary creation in our theological understanding.

Weltanschauung

The German word for world-view, the way in which we understand the world we live in and our place in it.

References

The following abbreviations refer to the volumes of Teilhard's works referred to in the book; unless otherwise indicated the publishers are Wm Collins and Son, London and the date given is that of the publication of the English translation.

PM   *The Phenomenon of Man*, translated by Bernard Wall et al. 1965 (Fontana edition)

MD   *The Divine Milieu*, translated by Bernard Wall et al. 1964 (Fontana edition)

HU   *Hymn of the Universe*, translated by Gerald Vann, 1970 (Fontana edition)

FM   *The Future of Man*, translated by Norman Denny 1964

AM   *The Appearance of Man*, translated by J.M. Cohen 1965

VP   *The Vision of the Past*, translated by J.M. Cohen 1966

MPN   *Man's Place in Nature*, translated by René Hague 1971 (Fontana edition)

WTW   *Writings in Time of War*, translated by René Hague 1968

SC   *Science and Christ*, translated by René Hague 1968

HE   *Human Energy*, translated by J.M. Cohen

AE   *Activation of Energy*, translated by René Hague 1970

CE   *Christianity and Evolution*, translated by René Hague 1971

TF   *Toward the Future*, translated by René Hague 1975

HM   *The Heart of Matter*, translated by René Hague 1978

MM   *The Making of a Mind: Letters from a Soldier-Priest 1914–19*, translated by René Hague

LT   *Letters from a Traveller*, translated by René Hague et al. 1967 (Fontana edition)

LZ   *Letters to Leontine Zanta*, ed. R. Garric and H. De Lubac SJ, translated by Bernard Wall 1969

Below are the essays in the various volumes with the dates of writing-these references might be useful in locating the texts used in the Appendix.

The Heart of Matter

HM/NF	Nostalgia for the Front	September 1917
HM/GM	The Great Monad	15 January 1918
HM/MU	My Universe	14 April 1918
HM/NPG	Note on the Presentation of the Gospel in a New Age	January 1919
HM/NM	The Names of Matter	Easter 1919
HM/MAC	On My Attitude to the Official Church	5 January 1921
HM/MW	The Mass on the World	1923
HM/MIP	My Intellectual Position	April 1948
HM/HM	The Heart of Matter	30 October 1950
HM/C	The Christic	March 1955

Science and Christ

SC/HB	What exactly is the Human Body?	1919
SC/NUC	Note on the Universal Christ	January 1920
SC/SC	Science and Christ	27 February 1921
SC/MU	My Universe	25 March 1924
SC/PM	The Phenomenon of Man	September 1928
SC/CW	Christianity in the World	May 1933
SG/MUB	Modern Unbelief	25 October 1933
SC/RCW	Some Reflexions on the Conversion of the World	9 October 1936
SC/SM	The Salvation of Mankind	11 November 1936
SC/SHSC	Super-Humanity, Super-Christ, Super Charity	August 1945
SC/AC	Action and Activation	August 1946
SC/DSC	Degrees of Scientific Certainty in the Idea of Evolution	November 1946
SC/E	Ecumenism	December 1946
SC/RVR	The Religious Value of research	20 August 1947
SC/NBS	Note on the Biological Structure of Mankind	3 August 1948

SC/WL	What is Life?	3 March 1950
SC/CB	Can Biology Enable us to Emerge into the Transcendent?	May 1951
SC/RWW	Research, Work and Worship	March 1955

Activation of Energy

AE/MC	The Moment of Choice	Christmas 1939
AE/AS	The Atomism of Spirit	13 September 1941
AE/RO	The Rise of the Other	20 January 1942
AE/UU	Universalisation and Union	20 March 1942
AE/C	Centrology	13 December 1944
AE/AL	The Analysis of Life	10 June 1945
AE/ODS	Outline of a Dialectic of Spiri	25 November 1946
AE/PT	The Place of Technology in a General Biology of Mankind	16 January 1947
AE/NPHS	On the Nature of the Phenomenon of Human Society & Its Hidden Relationship with Gravity	23 April 1948
AE/PCU	The Psychological Conditions of the Unification of Man	December 1948
AE/PCE	The Phenomenon of Counter-Evolution in Human Biology	26 January 1949
AE/SSM	The Sense of the Species in Man	31 May 1949
AE/ERW	The Evolution of Responsibility in the World	5 June 1950
AE/CRC	Reflections on Two Converse Forms of Spirit	25 July 1950
AE/ZL	The Zest for Living	November 1950
AE/SES	The Spiritual Energy of Suffering	8 January 1950
AE/MTP	A Mental Threshold Across Our Path:Cosmos To Cosmogenesis	15 March 1951
AE/RSP	Reflections on Scientific Probability	25 March 1951
AE/CU	The Convergence of the Universe	28 July 1951
AE/TCM	Transformation & Continuation in Man	19 November 1951

AE/MPA	A Major Problem for Anthropology	30 December 1951
AE/RE	The Reflection of Energy	27 April 1952
AE/RCM	Reflections on the Compression of Mankind	18 January 1953
AE/OLC	On Looking at a Cyclotron	April 1953
AE/EE	The Energy of Evolution	24 May 1953
AE/SU	The Stuff of the Universe	14 July 1953
AE/AHE	The Activation of Human Energy	6 December 1953
AE/DB	The Death Barrier and Co-Reflection	1 January 1955

Toward the Future

TF/SM	The Sense of Man	Feb.–March 1929
TF/RW	The Road of the Wes	8 September 1932
TF/EC	The Evolution of Chastity	February 1934
TF/FA	The Function of Art	13 March 1939
TF/AW	The Awaited Word	31 October 1940
TF?NCC	Note on the Concept of Christian Perfection	1942
TF/RH	Reflections on Happiness	28 December 1943
TF/MSW	Can Moral Science Dispense with Metaphysics	23 March 1945
TF/SCF	The Spiritual Contribution of the Far East	10 February 1947
TF/TP	Two Principles and a Corollary	February 1948
TF/MFV	My Fundamental Vision	26 August 1948
TF/MSC	Notes on the Mystical Sense	1951

Writings in Time of War

WTW/CL	Cosmic Life	17 May 1916
WTW/MWK	Mastery of the World & the Kingdom of God	20 September 1916
WTW/SM	Struggle Against the Multitude	Feb.–March 1917
WTW/MM	The Mystical Milieu	13 August 1917
WTW/CU	Creative Union	November 1917
WTW/SW	The Soul of the World	1918
WTW?EF	The Eternal Feminine	March 1918

WTW/P	The Priest	8 July 1918
WTW/OF	Operative Faith	28 September 1918
WW/FC	Forma Christi	22 December 1918
WTW/NUE	Note on the Universal Element	22 December 1918
WTW/PL	The Promised Land	February 1919
WTW/UE	The Universal Element	21 February 1919

Human Energy

HE/SE	The Spirit of the Earth	9 March 1931
HE/SPV	Significance & Positive Value of Suffering	1 April 1933
HE/SPU	Sketch of a Personalistic Universe	4 May 1936
HE/PS	The Phenomenon of Spirituality	March 1937
HE/HE	Human Energy	20 October 1937
HE/MS	The Mysticism of Science	20 March 1939

The Future of Man

FM/NP	A Note on Progress	10 August 1920
FM/SHP	Social Heredity and Progress	1938
FM/GO	The Grand Option	3 March 1939
FM/SRO	Some Reflections on Progress	30 March 1939
FM/NS	The New Spirit 1942	13 February 1942
FM/LP	Life and the Planets	10 March 1945
FM/PM	The Planetisation of Mankind	25 December 1945
FM/RSR	Reflections on Repercussions of the Atom Bomb	September 1946
FM/FP	Faith in Peace	January 1947
FM/FM	Faith in Man	8 March 1947
FM/RM	Reflections on the Rights of Man	22 March 1947
FM/HR	The Human Rebound of Evolution	20 April 1948
FM/TG	Turmoil or Genesis	20 December 1947
FM/DCF	The Directions and Conditions of the Future	30 June 1948

FM/EDI   The Essence of the Democratic
           Idea   2 February 1949
FM/MMB   Does Mankind Move Biologically
           upon Itself   4 May 1949
FM/HP   The Heart of the Problem   8 September 1949
FM/PCU   On the Probable Coming of an
           Ultra-Humanity   6 January 1950
FM/HU   Hope and Human
           Unanimisation   18 January 1950

Christianity and Evolution
CE/PHC   Note on the Physical Union between the
           Humanity of Christ and the Faithful   January 1920
CE/NCT   The Notion of Creative
           Transformation   1920
CE/NMDA The Modes of Divine Action in
           the Universe   January 1920
CE/FRG   Fall, Redemption and
           Geocentrism   July 1920
CE/HROS Possible Historical Representations
           on Original Sin   Easter 1922
CE/PC   Pantheism and Christianity   1923
CE/CE   Christology and Evolution
           Christmas   1933
CE/HIB   How I Believe   28 October 1934
CE/EC   On the Essence of Christianity   May 1939
CE/CEV   Christ the Evolver   8 October 1942
CE/ICL   Introduction to the Christian
           Life   9 June 1944
CE/SNT   Suggestions for a New Theology   11 November 1945
CE/ROS   Reflections on Original Sin   15 November 1947
CE/CP   The Christian Phenomenon   10 May 1950
CE/MM   Monogenism and Monophyletism   1950
CE/CG   What the World is Looking for
           from the Church   4 September 1952
CE/ZS   Contingence of the Universe   1 May 1953
CE/PIW   Sequel to the Problem of Human
           Origins   5 June 1953
CE/GE   The God of Evolution   25 October 1952

About the Author

Born in Aberdare, South Wales, Alan Sage, now retired, has worked in Further and Higher Education for more than 30 years. With a Master of Theology degree from Glasgow University, he has taught a wide range of topics in religious studies and theology. His particular interest is in the work of the French Jesuit priest-scientist whose theological and spiritual thinking he has introduced to various audiences including undergraduates and parish groups.